In Search of Maturity

In Search of Maturity

AN INQUIRY INTO PSYCHOLOGY, RELIGION, AND SELF-EDUCATION

BY

Fritz Kunkel, M.D.

New York

CHARLES SCRIBNER'S SONS

Distributed by
Scrivener & Co.
6007 Barton Ave.
Los Angeles 38

To

ELISABETH KUNKEL

PREFACE

In Search of Maturity is based on more than twenty years of psychotherapeutic work. It is not written, however, for experts in psychology; it is addressed to everyone puzzled by his own problems and confused by the riddles of the contemporary world. It attempts to describe and to explain the deviations of individuals and groups alike, and to chart the way out. The reader, however, should not expect a panacea, a new philosophy, or an "ism". The application of our psychology to history and politics is limited by the simple fact that we only study the inner life of individuals and groups. As soon as outer circumstances, the presence or absence of raw materials, industrialization and economics are involved, the psychological viewpoint, though it remains valid, is but one among many factors. The reader will find therefore only a new viewpoint to be added to his earlier picture of life.

The location of this new viewpoint may be described as the cross-roads of religion and psychology. Its essence is the "We-experience", a psychological reality which everyone can find within himself and which he may describe as his membership in the group, his sympathy, love or responsibility for his fellow-men—or, in more general terms, as his humanity. (That the We-experience is not to be confused with humanitarianism will be clear to the reader.)

All objections to this new "religious psychology" have

been based so far on the fact that its point of departure, the We-experience, does not lend itself to a clear-cut "scientific" definition. Therefore, say the critics, the We-psychology is unscientific, cannot be verified in laboratory experiments, and consequently cannot become part of our scientific view of reality. It is true that the We-Psychology is nearer to art than to science. Only the deviations and diseases of the human mind are proper objects of exact scientific research. The positive side of the human mind, its creativity, love, courage and faith, cannot be described, and —even more important—can neither be invoked nor controlled by scientific methods. But even the artistic viewpoint is inadequate to the problems of our psychology, if we intend to deal with the present predicaments of mankind.

We have to include two large fields of experience: the religious life, and the life of the unconscious. The We-experience, as we shall see, provides an approach to both of them. There is no experience of God without the experience of the human We-relationship. Nor is there any We-experience without the growth of consciousness. The more we love, the more unconscious energies are integrated into our conscious personality.

There are undeveloped primitive tendencies in every one's unconscious mind (the tendencies which help to create wars, revolutions, passions, crimes, neuroses and insanity). To approach and influence them on a larger scale is possible only if we have the insight and the courage of religious life. The need is so urgent, as the reader will see, that we may gladly risk the criticism of being mystics or idealists.

Some theologians, however, are afraid that our religious psychology may damage the traditional system of Christian doctrine. Indeed, they find it not "Christian" enough. To avoid a useless discussion about what is and what is not "Christian" enough it may be sufficient to call the We-Psychology a "theocentric" psychology, though the New Testament is one of its main sources, and the character of Jesus its central point of orientation.

Acknowledgments: The conclusions of the following presentation are largely based on well-known facts as discussed in psychotherapeutic literature. Sigmund Freud, Alfred Adler, and C. G. Jung should be mentioned as the teachers to whom I owe most. In the religious field, Reinhold Niebuhr, John Macmurray, and Gerald Heard have contributed considerably to the clarification of my thinking. In addition, I am indebted to the many friends who assisted in the literary revision of the manuscript. I wish to thank Harper & Brothers for permission to quote from *The Moffatt Bible: A New Translation.*

This is my first book written in English; all the others have been translations. I hope the style, though far from satisfactory, will convey more directly than was possible in translation the original meaning of my psychology.

F. K.

Los Angeles
1943

Table of Contents

Contents

xii   Contents

LIST OF DIAGRAMS

Part One

THE HISTORICAL SITUATION

I

AN INTRODUCTORY CASE

This book deals with religion, psychology and growth. To indicate the nature and scope of our problems we shall first describe an imaginary case which may demonstrate the different methods and goals used by the physician, the minister and the psychologist. Then we shall explore the actual relationship between these methods, their interdependence, as well as the possibilities of mutual assistance, with special emphasis on the contribution of psychology.

A burglar, whose specialty was scaling the outer wall of a building and entering the rooms through the windows, fell and broke his leg during an attempted theft. He had to be taken to a hospital where he lay depressed, worried, and almost sleepless, remembering several previous accidents which had occurred on similar occasions. The physician sensed that something was worrying his patient, but he hesitated to interfere with private affairs. The burglar said the accident had occurred at his home while he was mending the drain, but the story did not seem probable to the physician. Rumors circulated among the nurses concerning the suspicious-looking character who had brought the patient to the hospital at a very unusual hour.

3

When the physician mentioned these facts to the patient, he was told that the patient was there to have his leg treated, and not to be questioned about his private life. From then on, the physician carefully respected the limits of his profession. He did all within his power to heal the broken leg, and to give the patient special exercises which would restore its full use. At the end of the cure the burglar remarked, "You have certainly helped me; I feel more able than before to carry on my work."

The physician was right from the viewpoint of his professional ethics. He must improve health, remove pathological disturbances, and restore the full, unrestricted mastery of the body and mind without asking for what purpose they may be used. Except for a few dangerous cases, and especially epidemics, the social interest is not—or not yet—his business. He is, as it were, an employee, and his employer, the patient, tells him where the limits of his duties are to be found. In other words, the patient is free to fire the physician and hire another one.

When the hospital chaplain called, the physician told him of his suspicions regarding the man with the broken leg. The chaplain talked at length with the patient, finding him more approachable than he had anticipated. The man complained about restlessness, sleeplessness, and anxiety dreams. The chaplain suggested that the accident, and even more, the series of accidents which the patient had suffered, might indicate a crisis in his moral life, and that he should try to discover whether his attitude towards mankind and God was the right one. The burglar, after making sure that his secrets were safe under seal of the confessional, told the chaplain what his profession really was, and that he could not give it up for the reason that his family had to be supported. Burglary was his only skill and means of support; there was no alternative. The minister asserted that God would help him if he would give up his antisocial attitude, and the patient, honestly moved, asked to be prayed for. He told the minister quite frankly he was an illegitimate child, described all the miseries of a loveless childhood, cruel adolescence, and a hopeless struggle against unemployment; and finally admitted that his sleeplessness was due to his fear of being punished by supernatural justice.

It was a long, religious conversation. The chaplain felt, on leaving, that an erring soul had made a great step forward; while the burglar told himself—for the hundredth time in his life—that he would change his profession as soon as possible, hoping meanwhile that the Lord would grant him one more very successful burglary. But he knew that his prayer was not valid, and his sleep became more disturbed than ever. Further conversations with the chaplain convinced him more and more that he must change his life, but he could not find the way to bring this about.

The minister's approach is opposite to that of the physician. The latter receives the order to help from the patient. Therefore his ability to help is limited by the patient's will. The minister is commissioned by God and is, therefore, not limited by the patient's will to be helped. He can disturb the conscience of his client, can appeal to his fear of ultimate failure; and, if the patient is without faith, the minister can by his own faith arouse at least the suspicion that there may be a God. This is much more than the physician can achieve, but it does not reach the roots of evil. The average minister of the present time is an expert of light, but not of darkness. To deal with an intricate problem of darkness, he needs the help of depth psychology.

The burglar's anxiety dreams provided the opportunity for bringing the psychologist into the picture. Sometimes the physician himself may be a psychologist. In such a case he has to handle skillfully the double relationship— the medical one to the patient's body and consciousness, and the psychological one to his unconscious mind. The patient's unconscious will soon recognize him as the true helper, and this will give him a power and authority similar to that which the minister wields in the name of the Lord. In other cases the minister may be the psychologist, too, and this indeed is the ideal situation, because then his authority from above coincides with his authority from below, namely his capacity to move the powers of the unconscious. In our case, however, the psychologist was a friend and cooperator of both the physician and the minister.

After some discussion the psychologist was able to show the patient that there was a contradiction in his behavior. He wanted to do things, and he did not want to do them. He worked towards a goal, then unconsciously thwarted it. The results were blunders, forgetfulness, inner fear, insecurity and lack of coordination. As long as the inner conflict remained, one accident would follow another. The psychologist summed up: "Your heart is not in your work; either you must put your full heart into your work, or you must change your profession."

Now the burglar began to realize that he could not go on with his work. Neither morality nor fear of earthly and heavenly justice had provided a sufficient motive to change his career. But now he understood that his own unconscious aversion against his profession forced him to make mistakes, to produce failures, and in the end would compel him to give himself up.

His nights, now, were more sleepless than ever. Lying awake in the darkness, he began to see his life and the lives of his companions in a new light. To be a good burglar, one must be a bad man. There are very few good burglars, and none of them are perfect. There may be a very few bad men, and possibly not one of them is entirely bad. Thus—sooner or later—every burglar will make a mistake; his unconscious longing for goodness will frustrate the most ingenious crimes. Every criminal has his own traitor within himself. Either he must get rid of this traitor, this longing for righteousness, or his whole profession will collapse.

During the next consultations with the psychologist many remembrances from early childhood were revealed and the terrible hatred against his unknown father loomed above everything else. The whole later development of the burglar seemed to be a furious vengeance against this faithless father, who was said to have been a man of wealth. If this destructive energy could be used in a creative way, life would doubtless be a brilliant success.

"Revengefulness," said the psychologist, "is nearer to normality than burglary. But do not forget, revengefulness is a powerful poison. It will destroy you if you try to repress it, and it will destroy you if you express it in actions, as you have done so far. Don't repress it, or fight against it, or force yourself to be better than you are, for that is impossible. On the other hand, do not express it in crime, or fight against society as if society were your father; that cannot help you. There is only one way left —honesty. Honesty is the only virtue that you can employ at this moment, and it is the basis of all the other virtues which will develop later. This is the way. Confess honestly how much you hate your father, and how you would destroy him, inch by inch, if he were here." "Perhaps I wouldn't," said the burglar, "he is an old man now, I suppose, with trembling hands." "If he could know your fate," said the psychologist, "and what he did to your life, perhaps he would confess himself." "I hate him," said the burglar, "but I would . . . perhaps I would like to know him . . ."

So this amazing process, which we call catharsis or clarification, began. It begins with the decision not to fight against our vices, not to run away from them nor conceal them, but to bring them into the light; and this decision enables us to confess. Nobody can truly and thoroughly confess as long as he judges, condemns, excuses, or praises himself. In so doing he will repress or forget the most important part of his past, and therefore never discover the truth. But if his desire to be honest is greater than his desire to be good or bad, then the terrific power of his vices will become manifest, and behind the vice the old forgotten fear will turn up (the fear of being excluded from life), and behind the fear the pain (the pain of not being loved), and behind this pain of loneliness the deepest and most powerful and most hidden of all human desires: the desire to love, to give oneself, and to be part of the living stream that we call brotherhood. And the very moment that love is discovered behind hatred, all hatred disappears. The transmutation of power is brought about by the discovery of truth. But truth cannot be taught in words. It must actually be experienced within our own hearts. Furthermore, it cannot be experienced without confession, and confession needs a confessor who becomes the guide throughout suffering, fear, anxiety, anguish and pain. Dante could not go through hell without Virgil. Such is the task of the psychologist.

This kind of depth psychology is not only difficult, but dangerous too. The burglar may plead guilty not only for himself, but for his father as well. He may understand that his father could not help betraying the illegitimate child, just as the child could not help becoming a criminal. This father suffered from lack of love from his own father. It is always the same from generation to generation, throughout history; lack of love creates fear, greediness, darkness, loneliness, and hatred. The children bear the consequences of their parents' sins.

A client's confession becomes an ardent accusation, first against his parents, then his whole ancestry, and finally against life and creation. Who can help to overcome this ocean of suffering, except God himself? Where does the psychologist find the courage to assert and to prove that there is more light than darkness, and that there is a way out even for the burglar whose father was unable to love?

It is possible only on religious grounds. "God wants you," the psychologist says, "whether you understand his purpose or not. He calls you as he called your father and grandfather; and he will call your son, even if he is a deserter in the fourth generation. Our complaints are trifles compared with the innumerable mistakes we make every day. Now we begin to see the mistakes. Should we not try to prevent ourselves and our fellowmen from going on in the wrong direction?"

Here the psychologist becomes a priest, fighting not for the client's individual welfare, but rather for the Kingdom of Heaven. The interest shifts from the individualistic, earthly viewpoint to the metaphysical viewpoint of a universal religion. And here the psychologist, the minister and the physician need each other. The physician's pathological insight, especially with regard to the glandular system, the theologian's knowledge and experience of light and grace, the psychologist's capacity to dig out the very roots of darkness (he is the expert of sin and therefore in our days the best father confessor)—these three men's skill and wisdom must fuse into one united effort to help mankind. And this can be done only on the unifying basis of faith. Our Religious Psychology may be one of the means to attain this cooperation.

II

RELIGION WITHOUT PSYCHOLOGY

The history of our culture is largely characterized by the differentiation of occupations, professions, and sciences. In early times the chieftain of the tribe was king, priest, judge and physician. Later we find the religious power and the political power in opposition to each other. King and priest became competitors, but the priest continued to wield the entire power of the spirit. He continued to be the astrologer, the sorcerer, the physician, and, we may add, the scientist of the nation.

In Greek and Roman culture it is significant that philosophers, poets, lawyers and finally physicians drew away from religious tradition and began to criticize and, in part, to replace the priests. In the early Middle Ages, however, these powers again were integrated in the Church; and the process of differentiation then began anew. State and Church once more became rivals, and finally religion renounced all political aspiration. The Kingdom of Heaven, it was admitted, was not of this world.

During the Renaissance, philosophy and science fought their wars of independence. Even the arts broke away from the Church. During the seventeenth century, Christianity found itself limited to special rites at special occasions. Sunday was set aside for the Lord; but the political, economic, scientific, and technical development of western civilization was proceeding on its way during the week, without much regard for Christian faith, or even for Christian morality. Accordingly, the progress in science and art lost all relation to its religious origin. The human intellect seemed to be a secular force capable of development without the influence of religion.

The newest branches which emerged out of the unfolding tree of science, namely psychology and sociology, were almost unaware of the fact that religion and theology had handled the human soul and human society for countless centuries. The prophets of the Old Testament were practical sociologists. Jesus of Nazareth was the greatest psychologist of all times. But the riches of tradition, accumulated in religious literature and art, were neglected, and theology made no attempt to fight. It gave in, ignoring for many years the new sciences as they in turn ignored theology. Later, however, the ministers began to realize that they needed more knowledge of the human mind, as well as of social relations. So they began to study the secular psychology and sociology as they found them—instead of creating their own Christian sociology and psychology and teaching their secular colleagues the deeper truth and the stronger power that was entrusted to Christianity from the beginning.

There was growing social suffering, and a pagan like Karl Marx had to appear—and work out a wrong way of salvation; there was increasing individual suffering, and again a pagan like Sigmund Freud had to appear to show a wrong way of salvation. Why did not the Christian Church, the guardian of the human soul and social relationships, produce another Amos, Saint Paul, or Augustine to show the way out? Theology could withdraw from natural science, philosophy, and even art; but to surrender the fields of psychology and sociology was a strategic error that almost sealed the universal defeat of Christianity.

We must make up for this mistake, or Christianity will die out. The human mind is the central domain of religious life. We should not claim that we are the only experts who understand this field and are allowed to work in it; we should be grateful if other experts from different viewpoints share in our research; but we should be able to demonstrate that Christians know more about human life, human personality and human society than their secular fellow-research men. It should be a free and fair competition in which the spiritual power of Christianity could show its creativeness. We should admire all the great sociologists and psychologists, learn from them, but do better than they. If the Christian viewpoint is true, then it must lead both to theoretical knowledge and to practical findings. It cannot remain other-worldly. If it is true, it has to work in practical life and validate itself.

No miracle, no magic is required. The "power of the Lord" must compete neither with the physical energies explored by the scientists, nor with the vitamins used by the physician. But in the proper field where faith and despair, love and hatred, loyalty and betrayal are concerned, there both the Christian psychologist and the Christian sociologist should understand more fully, be more efficient and more successful than their pagan competitors. Otherwise, theology will remain in the stratosphere, and Christendom will collapse on earth.

*   *   *

One may safely say, however, that many of the great leaders in Church life have been great psychologists, and that some of them have expressed their insight into the human mind in an unforgettable way. The first of them —after Jesus himself—was Saint Paul with his confession, "The good that I would, I do not, but the evil which I would not, that I do." This famous statement is really the beginning of depth psychology. And there are others, like Saint Augustine, who followed Saint Paul in the attempt to explore the paradoxical reactions of the human soul.

But we find no adequate further development of this tendency. There are thousands of valuable observations, all through the centuries, but they remain casual, scattered and inconsistent. The average minister since the Reformation has had to rely on his own common sense and on superficial traditions as far as his efforts in helping people were concerned. His training in theology was thorough, but in handling individual cases his training was insufficient. The Roman Catholic Church has preserved more of its old pastoral experience in different kinds of exercises and retreats. But no creative evolution has followed. Thus the practical Christian workers had to be and to remain dilettantes and amateurs in psychology. Only the past ten years have shown the beginning of a change in this deplorable condition. But before we discuss the change, let us examine in some detail the results of this Christian limitation.

Take an example: a flood may occur. The theologian may think deeply about the unsolvable problem, as to how far floods can be understood as punishment for human sin. In the meantime the engineers build up a flood control, and the religious problem, at least in this special application, disappears. The theologian was right in not being too quick in drawing conclusions.

There is unemployment, and the theologian is faced with the same problem. The engineers of society, the economists and sociologists, try to help, but they are less successful than the engineers in the case of the flood. Unemployment increases. Mankind begins to look around for help, as did Nebuchadnezzar when his Scribes could not decipher the flaming inscription on the wall. Daniel alone could read it. Should not Christianity have anything to say about unemployment, social justice and reform? Is there no Daniel to decipher the "Mene tekel"?

The social gospel arose, but this again was Christianity without psychology. Human life was discussed without exploring man's real nature. Theologians studied sociology and economics, but they did not study the unconscious anxiety of the human mind. They did not understand why human beings are longing for improvement but resent every change. People want new life, but are afraid to give up their old lives. Theology knew this, but was unable to investigate its deeper meaning, and therefore even the social gospel, as seen from the psychological viewpoint, was mere theologism and doomed to failure.

There are nervous diseases and innumerable symptoms which arise from wrong habits and wrong character attitudes. If people complained about these symptoms, the ministers were supposed to send them to the doctor or to the psychologist. With proud modesty, they confined themselves to mere "religious" problems, considering it unethical towards physicians and consulting psychologists to encroach on their fields. "Imagine," said one of my patients in such a case, "that Saint Peter or Saint John had said to the lame man at the gate of the temple: 'Silver and gold have I none, and such as I have I cannot give thee because it would be unethical towards the physicians of Jerusalem.'" That would have been the beginning of theologism.

One of the powerful reactions against this pious sin of omission was the mushroom growth of Christian Science. Yet the counterswing in the opposite direction showed the same exclusiveness and one-sidedness as the swing itself. Christian Science, not allowing for medical and psychological research, shows even more the characteristics of theologism than the different theologies on the opposite side.

Theologism is the tendency to relate events of history and the problems of individual life directly to the highest entities. All intermediate links are left out. The inductive method of science which relates single facts to larger conceptions and the larger conceptions to still larger ones, is replaced by its opposite, the deductive method. The central idea of God or devil, light or darkness, is immediately applied to floods and unemployment, or headaches and sleeplessness. The only intermediate links that may be mentioned are sin and virtue, and if a virtuous person dies from cancer, this fate must prove that after all he was not virtuous enough. Here theologism turns into moralism and becomes even less efficient.

If the Christian helper were to follow the inductive method he would discover, for instance, that the headache is the adequate expression of an unconscious emotional tension, and that fear, envy, and competition are its basis. Envy always means that the envious person has not yet lived his full and real life. Behind the vice we find the unconscious virtue, the undeveloped possibility. The headache points to the sin of the buried talent. Theologism involves an arbitrary jumping from the periphery into the center, and back from the center to the periphery, with no consideration for the long and complicated way of distorted radii. Theologism, therefore, is in itself a sin of omission.

The results of this sin are dangerous. People with character difficulties, moral deviations and vices, are sent to the doctors as though they were sick. The physical and mental diseases certainly belong to the realm of medicine, and therefore the ethical evaluation in these cases must be avoided. But if vices are diseases, they cease to be vices; and theology, sending the drunkard and the gambler to the physician, relinquishes its last connection with reality: the ethical task.

When the thunderbolts of enthusiastic revivalists failed more and more, Christians finally became convinced that they needed another kind of help. They turned to medical psychology instead of developing their own resourcefulness and generating the much-needed religious psychology. On Sunday morning the minister preached that sexual perversions are the result of sin, according to Saint Paul. And on Monday he had to tell his clients that their nervous symptoms, including their perversions, were related to the Oedipus complex; they were a neurosis, but not a sin. This was what the minister had learned from modern psychology. And he soon realized that he had to choose between ministry and this kind of psychology. Thus he chose Christ—and left the clients whom he could not help to the psychoanalysts. The analysts told them triumphantly that the Church was wrong, and that Saint Paul was wrong; but they, the analysts, likewise failed to help them.

The situation grew from bad to worse. The serious neuroses, hysteria major, and grave compulsions, should obviously be sent to the expert psychotherapist. However, there is no doubt that minor nervous symptoms such as restlessness, sleeplessness, sleepiness, over- or underdeveloped sexual desires and numerous other disturbances occur not only in real neuroses. They are, in countless cases, the adequate expression for the normal crisis, as it happens and should happen in every human life.

When the self-sufficient philosophy fails, and the proud resourcefulness of modern life breaks down—in individual life or in group life—the inner crisis begins. Then it is normal for a normal person to react in an abnormal way. This is the great chance for the individual, and for Christianity. It is the moment when new life and new faith could be born. But if you mistake the labor pains of the human soul for a mental disease, and send the suffering person to the wrong kind of midwife, the spiritual miscarriage is unavoidable. Who knows how many thousands or perhaps millions of prospective Christians have been turned away by the Church because their troubles were called "nervous symptoms"?

We must later consider in detail what usually happens to these persons. Here it may suffice to mention that the unconscious spiritual hunger which, in the last analysis, can be found behind most of the nervous symptoms, finally finds its fulfillment in cheap and strange pseudo-religions, if the real granary is closed because of the incompetence of its officialdom. Christianity is then replaced by old superstitions, imported from the East and West; or by skillfully advertised substitutes such as misunderstood yoga practice on the one side, and on the other, shallow fortune-telling at the street corner. These are the results of the sin of omission which we call religion without psychology.

Religion Without Psychology

III

PSYCHOLOGY WITHOUT RELIGION

Throughout the nineteenth century we find innumerable attempts, outside the Church, to explore and use the forces of the human mind which were neglected during the seventeenth and eighteenth centuries. Movements such as Mesmerism, Hypnotism, Couéism, and New Thought are the outstanding examples. None of them has achieved the position which they claimed, but all of them have proved that there are hidden energies in the deeper layers of the human mind which may give a terrific power to those who could evoke them.

Whenever these forces were revealed in earlier times, they were thought to be demons, gods, or devils. The priests were supposed to understand them and to deal properly with them. And the ancient Church was able to do so to a certain extent.

Then, between the fifteenth and eighteenth centuries, the youthful and arrogant natural sciences decided that there were no such things as ghosts, devils, or gods. And just as the priests refused to look through the telescope for fear of seeing something that might destroy their cosmology, the scientists refused to observe hypnotism and telepathy for fear of endangering their mechanistic vision of life. This time the Christian Church stood on the side of science. Most ministers disbelieved in ghosts, angels, or devils, and in prophetic dreams, in spite of all the evidence in the Bible.

The new movements which dealt with the hidden depths of the human mind (or even the universal mind) were essentially experimental and practical. When they finally began to search for a theoretical or philosophical explanation of their findings, they found themselves ostracized by scientists and theologians alike. Therefore they remained outsiders, and developed the most fantastic philosophies of their own. Later the Church felt justified in stating: "Was it not right to reject them? It is paganism, superstition, and irreverence; therefore the whole idea must be a delusion."

The theory was condemned, and the facts on which the theory was based were neglected. But the hidden forces continued to disturb the quiet placidity of mankind, of natural science, and theology. Diseases and suffering, insanity in individuals as well as in large groups, crime and perversion, in fact all the vices that Saint Paul described in his letter to the Romans, tortured the helpless nations, Christian and pagan—and there was no help for them. Saint Paul had written his letter in vain.

During the first World War, it became increasingly evident that the bloody convulsions would drag on unless a remedy was discovered and applied which could influence the deeper layers of the human character where the disturbances apparently originated. Many people were aware that not only was religion at stake, but that the problem in itself was a religious one. Religious practice, however, was unable to reach those deeper layers.

As early as 1900, Sigmund Freud had discovered the "unconscious." He was able to present so much evidence, and to describe his discovery in such "scientific" language, that the scientific world, after some grudging hesitation, finally accepted the facts. But the theoretical superstructure was, in accordance with the time and circumstances, a rather poor naturalistic, even mechanistic, philosophy; and therefore Christianity, with very few exceptions, again condemned the ideas together with the facts. In Christian life there was no "unconscious" until the first World War was over. Theology rejected Freud, and Freud rejected religion. To him Christianity was an illusion.

In the meantime Alfred Adler had emphasized the unity of the human individual, in defiance of the multiform and impersonal structure which the Freudians believed they had discovered. This was more acceptable to Christianity. The Adlerian teachings were used here and there in Christian work, though the teacher himself was an idealistic non-believer to whom religion was a neurotic state of mind. But Adler's "Individual Psychology" was not "Depth-psychology" in the proper sense of the word. Adler ignored the deeper unconscious layers and therefore did not reach the destructive and demoniac forces which endangered our proud civilization.

Marxism, then coming into the foreground, pretended to know something about the origin of these forces, but this was an error. Where Marxism was applied, the same will to power, private and collective, the same recklessness and competition (not economic but political), tore to shreds the human society, just as they had done during the domination of the bourgeoisie.

Finally it became clear, at least to some observers, that Christianity only was in possession of the key which would unlock the door to new life and new culture, both for the individual and for nations. But the key did not yet work. The people to whom it was entrusted evidently did not know how to use it. They knew the key, but they did not know the lock, and consequently were unable to enter the basement of the human mind where the powerful dynamos operated. Mankind was afraid of its own high voltage, and nobody knew how to deal with its power.

At that time, C. G. Jung had unfolded his "Analytical Psychology." He knew enough about the lock that held the deeper layers; he even knew something about the dynamos, and how to transform the high voltage. His theories are not mechanistic, and only to a small extent, naturalistic. As a matter of fact, they are becoming more and more Christian.

Jung's point is that the power stations in the human unconscious mind are not individual qualities, as the individualist, Sigmund Freud, still assumed. They are collective powers, controlling large numbers of individuals, and in the hands of reckless dilettantes they may easily destroy nations, countries, and even races. To deal with them is partly a problem of knowledge, and this knowledge must be depth-psychology. But it is at the same time a religious mission, and it may lead to the crucifixion of the missionaries who attempt to descend into the unconscious power stations of mankind.

As long as depth-psychologists were not religious, they were startled by their terrible discoveries. They found in history and in the life of contemporaries powerful unconscious motives which they called "the images of the great leader, the sorcerer, the witch, the madonna." They understood that what is now happening to our civilization cannot be described as error, ambition, greed, or war hysteria. It is much more than all these—it is a change in the unconscious structure of the human mind.

What this change actually means in the last analysis, and how it can be controlled—these questions transcend the realm of psychology. No science will ever be able to answer them. Here is the place where religious conviction, faith, and mission, should enter. If they do enter, the intersection of depth-psychology and religion may prove to be the starting point of a new Christian culture.

IV

COLLABORATION OF
RELIGION AND PSYCHOLOGY

The collaboration of religion and psychology must be based on the unanimous conviction of both parties that man is not as he should be. This presupposition limits us on the side of psychology to the so called "depth-psychology." The different schools of this psychology, as well as all Christian theology, subscribe to the statement that man as we now know him is not "normal," if norm means what he ought to be. Academic psychology, which takes the average man as the normal man, excludes itself, at least for the time being, from our common religious endeavor.

Only our conviction that man should be changed, and that history without the inner change of mankind will end in chaos, gives us the right starting point for research and action. The insight that man was on the wrong path religiously, and the discovery of the better way, was the starting point of the Reformation. The insight that our unconscious powers are going astray, and the discovery that we can help them to find the better way by bringing them into consciousness, is the origin of religious psychology, and at the same time it is the beginning of the psychological period of religion.

Psychology, however, including the deepest kind of depth-psychology, cannot rescue us without the help of religion. It is doomed to deteriorate into mere psychologism, just as theology without psychology deteriorates into theologism. The depth is lost and only platitudes remain. Such a platitude, for instance, is the Freudian idea that art is "nothing but" sublimated libido, or that God is "nothing but" the father image projected onto the universe. Religion, in that case, would be explained as deriving from certain psychological forces or forms. It is secondary and not genuine in itself. These statements are pseudo-scientific errors, ignoring the depth of reality.

Psychologism claims to explain and to cure all disturbances, but it fails except in simple cases which can be cured by any psychologist or quack. Let us suppose that some one has to die, either by cancer or the firing squad, and has two weeks in which to prepare for this ordeal. Here psychologism must fail. Religion without psychology would be of some help, but ultimately only religious psychology and psychological religion can adequately meet the problem. If we consider the tasks of ministry and counseling as broad and as deep as reality presents them to us, we will discover that psychologism is even worse than theologism.

A good example is the treatment of anxiety. Psychologism would hold that anxiety, in the last analysis, is based on error. Forces or desires have gone erroneously astray. The original error must be dug out of the unconscious (perhaps the patient was left alone at night when a child), and the adult client will go through this experience again in his dreams and his imagination, understanding that there is no reason for anxiety. In some cases this kind of cure is sufficient, the symptoms disappear and a new adjustment is possible. But in many cases, fortunately, the symptoms do not disappear, or they are replaced by other symptoms. Then the cure must go on, and we find that the client is right and the psychologist is wrong.

The better representatives of depth-psychology, especially the Jungian School, would know that the error is a deeper one. Anxiety—as well as hatred—is love turned into the negative. We must learn to tolerate, to accept, and finally to love the thing or person, the symbol or spirit of which we are afraid. Sustain the horror, kiss the monster, as Jesus kissed Judas—that will redeem the negative power and transmute it into positive power. Anxiety will be turned into love and creativity. This development, if it can be accomplished, will cure the patient in many cases. But sometimes it cannot be done, sometimes it does not help, for the very reason that there is ample cause for being anxious.

The situation of man, our strange dual citizenship in the realms of the spirit and of nature, may indeed cause bewilderment and fear. All non-religious depth-psychology, as well as the shallow psychologism, fails to understand man's futile and dangerous position. It does not see that there is a deeper kind of anxiety, not representing the negative aspect of human relationship but the negative relationship to God; and therefore it cannot help.

The little child was afraid of something very real, very true, but not yet understood: the futility and loneliness of man. The presence of the parents would have postponed the issue until the child was mature enough to meet it. But in his precocious loneliness the child had to face the insoluble problem ten years too early. Now, thirty years later, the psychologist and the client together must face it; and that is possible only on religious grounds. Without faith no depth-psychology can be useful; it may even be harmful in many cases. A new and real and true relationship to God is the only way out.

We need faith. The more we understand the predicament of mankind, expressed by the intricate darkness of the deeper layers of the unconscious, the more we need the light and the power which are stronger than all individual and collective forces of evil. We need a knowledge of human nature which transcends our scientific and artistic theories. We have many hints pointing to this knowledge in mythology and philosophy and in non-Christian religions. But we have only one book which gives us the full description of the human situation, and of the way leading through all troubles and frustrations, and finally into utmost light. It is the great textbook of depth-psychology: the New Testament. Without this religious knowledge, we cannot cure the more serious cases of anxiety and compulsive neuroses. We cannot help the dying person to face death, and we cannot hope to master the collective dark powers which threaten human culture today.

V

RELIGIOUS PSYCHOLOGY

As a matter of fact, the collaboration between psychology and religion has developed rapidly during the last ten years. Today there are hundreds of religious workers in counseling, in group work, or in the "cure of souls" who use psychology. They take what they think suitable from all the various schools of psychology with which they are familiar. An increasing number of books are attempting to adjust the discoveries of depth-psychology to the special tasks of Christian ministry. However, the results achieved with the tools that are available so far are not at all encouraging, and there is a growing realization on the part of Christian workers of the need for new and different psychological tools. And on the other hand there can be no doubt among experts, nowadays, that considerable and creative powers can be released from the unconscious, and that they will work in constructive ways if the synthesis between psychology and religious life is achieved.

The most serious obstacle to our endeavor is to be found in a simple and common misunderstanding. Psychology is considered a natural science. Observations of facts, tests, experiments, statistics are used, and logical conclusions are drawn exactly as they are in the fields of physics or chemistry. This kind of psychology, of course, can be taught to every one. All people, Buddhists and Christians, materialists and idealists, would then be forced to accept the same irrefutable scientific truths about the human mind or psyche or soul. Under this system there should be only one true psychology throughout the universe, just as there is only one true physics. Actually, however, there are almost as many psychologies as there are psychologists. Each psychologist speaks his own language, discovers his own facts, and gives his own interpretations. And this situation will continue just as long as psychology is held to be a natural science, instead of being given its rightful place as an historical or philosophical science, together with ethics, economics, and the history of culture.

In a science like physics every new discovery must augment the existing body of knowledge. It may force us to change the earlier theories to a certain extent, but it would never create a new kind of physics in addition to the one which exists. In psychology it is different. Adler's discovery could not be assimilated into the Freudian system. It had to become the basis of a new system of its own. And what Jung discovered could not be understood or even seen from Adler's or Freud's viewpoint. His psychology includes most of the facts which his forerunners described. But his philosophical approach is incompatible with theirs. This fact can be understood as an historical necessity if we admit that psychology is a "philosophical science." Its viewpoint depends on the scientist's conscious or unconscious philosophy. Therefore it must change with the changing phases of human culture. The one psychology for which we are searching will be the result of the team-work of many psychologists who share the same viewpoint. But it will be opposed to the psychologies which arise from different viewpoints.

In this way materialism has produced another kind of psychology than has idealism. Thinking in terms of cause and effect, and using the preservation of energy as an underlying concept, the materialists discovered "l'homme machine." Life was a mechanism. This discovery left no place for free decisions and responsibility, and therefore led to complete determinism and pessimism. There was neither good nor evil, since even a broken machine still obeyed the natural laws. Life was a blind interplay of forces, meaningless, valueless, and dull. The last and greatest exponent of this psychology was Sigmund Freud.

The idealist is convinced beforehand that "man is good." The connection of means and goals explains human life to him. There would be no evil or suffering if man could only understand that all men are good. Evil is an error and can be overcome by better education. This psychology is essentially rationalistic and optimistic. Its last great exponent was Alfred Adler.

At this point the objection is made that such a controversy can be resolved only by objective investigation and observation of facts, according to the rules of natural science. But this is not true, fortunately and unfortunately. If it were true, life would be much simpler and less dangerous, but on the other hand less colorful and exciting, and totally uncreative.

Suppose a man, let us say a teacher, has had trouble with

his supervisor in the morning. He could not fight back and had to repress his anger. When he came home in the evening he found that his wife was ten minutes behind schedule and that dinner was not ready. Now his anger explodes and he feels that his impatience is caused not so much by the late dinner and his wife's tardiness, as by his encounter with the supervisor much earlier in the day. Is this not an exact instance of the law of preservation of energy? The emotion repressed in the morning remains buried in the unconscious and rises to consciousness as soon as circumstances permit. Apparently Freud is right and Adler is wrong.

But now suppose that when the teacher comes home, he finds a letter from his editor telling him that his last article was an excellent contribution, and that letters of appreciation are pouring in from all over the country. His reaction is quite different. "Darling," he cries, "read this letter! What a fool that supervisor was this morning to tell me that I cannot teach." He does not even notice that the dinner is late. Is this not an exact instance of ego-evaluation? His ego was defeated in the morning, and re-elated in the evening. No problem of energy is involved. Everything is explained in terms of means and goals; the chief goal being self-esteem. Apparently Adler is right and Freud is wrong.

We can find ample "evidence" for all our theories. Most psychological observations lend themselves to different interpretations, and frequently even the "facts" are visible only from a certain viewpoint, remaining invisible to the observer who looks from the opposite side. Religious experiences in particular can rarely be verified, and certainly cannot be understood by irreligious psychologists. The autobiography of a man like Saint Augustine is to men like Freud and Adler, what a painting by Raphael would be to a blind man. But critics of painting should not be blind. A tone-deaf person cannot write the philosophy of music, and a non-religious psychologist cannot explain experiences of faith and conversion, darkness and light. If he tries to do so, he is doomed to produce only platitudes; he is in the position of one who tries, on a two-dimensional plane, to investigate a three-dimensional structure. This is the meaning of the word "platitude".

Christian life must and will produce religious psychology, just as the materialistic period produced Freudian psychoanalysis, and as the short interlude of idealism after the first World War expressed itself in the Adlerian Individual Psychology.

It is inevitable that the Christian psychologist should look at the "objects" of his research from the Christian viewpoint. To him, anxiety is the expression of the distance between God and man. He understands that sometimes religion is, as Freud said, an "illusion," and, more frequently, as Adler said, an "escape." But he knows too that in both cases the religious development may lead through illusions and escapes and failures and disappointments to the ultimate discovery of truth, to the experience of faith and to the creativeness given by grace. To him, evil and suffering are not just the "wrecked machine" of the materialist, or the "error" of the idealist. They are these and more: they are the dynamics of human life forcing man to recognize the deficiencies and perils of his situation, and compelling him to struggle with all his might for what he cannot achieve by his own endeavor alone—his way through darkness to light.

The more we understand that our neurotic symptoms are expressions of hatred, fear, and lack of love, and realize that hatred, fear, and lack of love in one generation produce the same attitudes in the next, the more vividly we realize that neither education nor social reform, nor yet political change, can eradicate our suffering. Suffering, evil, deviations, and character difficulties (not only in neurotics, but in all "normal" people) will continue and will increase until mankind finds the religious solution. Socialism does not cure egocentricity. Sexual satisfaction does not erase lack of love. Both Psychoanalysis and Individual Psychology fall short. Religious psychology is necessary.

This being true, again the question arises as to why Christian workers have to pick up little psychological insights and partial truths here and there. Why has nobody thus far provided a real and practical system of Christian psychology? Probably the deepest reason for this is to be found in a general mistake on the part of Christendom itself: namely, in its approach to the problem of sin. Vices, character difficulties, and nervous symptoms are said to be related to sin, and sin is only to be shunned, never to be discussed or investigated. Sin is bad, and the good man turns away in horror. This emotional attitude is one of the gross fallacies of theology, whether it takes itself out in indignation or pity. We psychologists know that this attitude betrays the deficiencies of the Christian workers themselves. The individual worker has not yet solved his own problems; therefore he cannot solve the problems of his clients. He calls them terrible sins, and turns them over to the Holy Ghost.

Suppose a surgeon were to turn away in disgust when he discovered a large cancer in full growth. Is not his ability as a helper dependent on his eagerness to study the disease, to investigate its nature and origin, and to find a possible cure? And this in spite of the terrible aspect and unbearable odor? Only when we have learned to do the same with vices and deficiencies and nervous symptoms can we really be of help. Like those Christian missionaries who work with the sick and the criminal, or the poor of the slums and underprivileged areas, we have to become experts of sin, darkness, and suffering. We need a microscope for the microbes of darkness.

The Christian psychologist must face the intricacies of the dark power, and explore its hiding places in the unconscious of himself and his fellowmen. Neither academic research, with all its experiments and statistics, nor pagan depth-psychology, with all its experience and partial success, can give us the knowledge and the courage needed for this task. Only a genuinely religious psychology is adequate.

VI

THE RELIGIOUS VIEWPOINT

Many different systems of academic psychology and at least three kinds of depth-psychology have been offered to the suffering world during the last forty years. A large number of psychological terms have been used and are being used in every-day language without regard for the system or the background which they presuppose. People talk of inhibitions, repressions, projections, and inferiority complexes without knowing that by doing so they are using very different viewpoints and incompatible philosophies. Many psychologists attempt to analyze the same cases for a certain time in the Freudian way, then apply the Adlerian terminology, and finally interpret dreams according to Jung.

This proves that all the different systems contain some truth and are useful to a certain extent; on the other hand it proves that even psychologists are not aware of the deeper implications and philosophical consequences of the different terms. They propagate determinism when they use Freudian language, and indeterminism when they follow Adler. Sooner or later the unconscious of their clients faces them with the contradictory consequences of their conflicting methods, and the cure stops before they have reached the decisive point.

This confusion of languages should be avoided, but it is better than the exclusive use of one consistent terminology of a one-sided school. The psychologist who goes through this experience of changing aspects and changing terminologies will learn at least one very important fact, namely, that psychological truth is deeper than language. What is real in our inner experience may be called "libido" or "energy" or "will to power" or the "power of the Lord." All the big words point to certain aspects of the truth; but the truth itself, the inner reality as such, cannot be touched by them. This experience protects us against the usual mistake of the beginner who confuses the real thing with its psychological name. The Freudian student discovers an Oedipus complex and thinks it is something real. The Jungian describes the same reality, and even a little more, as the fear of the Great Mother. This seems to be a different reality, but just as real as the Oedipus complex. Both are right in so far as their words point to certain attitudes of certain ineffable powers. Both are wrong in so far as they feel that they have found *the* truth.

The psychologist should be able to talk the language of Freud and Adler as easily as the language of Jung and the We-Psychology. Then he will know that every fact can be looked upon from different angles, and that no terminology conveys the whole truth. More important, however, is his understanding of the philosophical viewpoint which lies hidden behind the terminology. And if he is open-minded enough, he will discover that neither the mechanistic view of Freud, nor the idealistic view of Adler, can give him the leverage to move the deeper problems of the human mind.

All monistic systems of psychology break down before the simple and paradoxical fact that man is free as a spirit, and at the same time determined as a body. So far life seems to be dualistic. It seems to consist of spirit and body. At least it can be discussed from the physical viewpoint, and from the spiritual viewpoint. On the other hand, it is one and indivisible. Man is not body plus spirit; he is a unit beyond both. He lives at the same time in the spiritual and in the physical atmosphere, just as he lives in space and time without being divided into a space-being and a time-being. Every action being one and indivisible expresses itself, as it were, in two different languages. Something happens in the spiritual world: a decision is made, responsibility is established, either love or hatred increases, either light or darkness is helped. And something happens in the physical world too. A letter is written, or a car is driven, or a house is built. But the action is one. The decision without the letter is nothing, as is the letter without the decision. The one indivisible action is the decision expressed in the letter. Human life is one, and it is neither mere physical nor mere spiritual existence, it is more than both.

This viewpoint, being dualistic and monistic at the same time, is the Christian viewpoint. It is, so far as we can see, nearer to truth than any other philosophy of life. And the psychology based on this viewpoint provides a better opportunity to describe and to understand and to influence human life than any other psychological system.

Having decided upon our philosophical viewpoint, we must probe into all the various factors connected with it. In addition to our own experiences and experiments we must examine the observations and discoveries of the different psychological schools, as well as their terms and definitions, with reference to our basic conception of human nature. If facts contradict this basic concept, the latter will have to be changed; and if terms interfere with it, the concept must be preserved, and the terms revised. Then the new terms should be applied to the facts, and if they cover and explain more of them, our procedure will be justified. If not, it must be improved.

In no case should any fact be omitted. Religious psychology must cover the whole field and include all the discoveries of previous psychological systems, or Christianity cannot be—as we claim—the highest and most mature of all philosophies and religions.

On the other hand, our psychology should remain partly an empirical science and partly an art. It should be the result of practical experiences, based on lessons and conclusions derived from the failures and successes in each day's work. At the same time it should be creative in applying its methods artistically, that is, with the spontaneous insight true to all genuine art.

The New Testament, as has already been stated, gives us this combined viewpoint of science and art, and furnishes us, moreover, with some very practical hints, even technical terms—such, for example, as the idea of suffering resulting from buried talents. The essential insight which distinguishes depth-psychology from academic psychology is stated once and forever by Jesus: "You are like tombs whitewashed; they look comely on the outside, but inside they are full of dead men's bones and all manner of impurity" (Mt. 23:27, Moffatt). The existence of our unconscious desires and our repressed tendencies could not be described more strikingly.

Our psychology, however, should not be restricted by dogmatic statements which have merely been derived from and are not immediately found in the New Testament nor by conventional interpretations of the New Testament itself. Our psychology needs a complete freedom of research, and, if our discoveries should lead to certain changes in interpretations and dogmatic conceptions, we should probably discover theologies and denominations which have defended already for centuries these "new" ideas of ours.

One more quality should be pointed out as being essential to our viewpoint. It must be dynamic, and not static. God is life; the human being should be alive; and the more alive he is the nearer he is to God. What life means in this connection has to be explored carefully; but for man, as long as he lives in time, it certainly includes change, growth, and development. Gradual evolution and catastrophic mutation can be equally alive. Stagnation and rigid preservation of a given state of development mean negative change, degeneration, decay, or death—and even decay and death are, in the last analysis, dynamic processes.

This dynamic view leads to far-reaching consequences. Intellectual understanding usually coincides with explaining the unknown by the known. A stone falls to the earth; this is the law of gravitation. The balloon soars, and apparently contradicts this law. If the upward movement can be retraced to gravitation (the air being heavier than the balloon) it is "understood." It takes us some time to understand, however, that we neither understand the balloon nor the falling stone, because gravitation is a mystery in itself. The most familiar things are the least comprehensible ones, if we use the word "comprehend" with sufficient exactness.

The "static" understanding of reality goes back not only from the unknown to the known, but also from the more complicated structure to the more simple—for example (in space) from the organism to the organ and from the organ to the cell; and (in time) from the later situation to the earlier one, that is, from the grown body to the embryo and from the embryo to the germ. Its method of thinking is limited to the relation of cause and effect. In psychology this way has failed completely. Psychology is possible only where the "static" view of life has been supplemented by the dynamic view.

Even physics, the most static of all sciences, has discovered that the most stable things are mere balances of forces. There are no imperishable substances in the world; the stone will one day be split into atoms, and the atoms into electrons, and what remains is energy, or more exactly, the interplay of conflicting energies. What these energies are, and why they move or do not move, nobody knows. Even in natural science, now, the known is dissolved into the unknown, and the static view is replaced by the dynamic view, and once more the familiar things become weird and incomprehensible, just as they were ten thousand years ago, when religion began.

Theology has always explained, or at least should have explained, the known by the unknown, the world by God, the creature by the Creator. Then the apparently simple becomes understandable by the apparently more complicated, and—most important of all—the past and the present will be interpreted by the future, just as the Old Testament has to be interpreted from the viewpoint of the New Testament. Creation presupposes purpose, valuation, ends. Not cause and effect, but the relation of means and goals, provide the adequate method for understanding human life and human history. Causality as an auxiliary method of thought can be used chiefly on the negative side to explain deficiencies and deviations. If a person does not love, there must be a cause for this lack. If he loves, he is moved not by a cause but by a goal.

The power which moves us to love, to strive, to create, is not working through the past. It is not a blind force, pushing us from behind, as the exploding gasoline pushes the piston of a motor. It is the creative power of the ultimate end, the value ahead of us in the infinite future, drawing us like a magnet, training us, transforming us like a breeder who transforms flowers into more beautiful flowers. This power creates and forms for its inconceivable purposes, and, if we resist or try to escape (placing our private ends against the ends of the universe), we are corrected and, if necessary, remolded as the potter remolds his clay.

Such is the religious viewpoint which allows us for the

first time in the history of science to work out a psychology applicable to individual life, and enables us at the same time to study and to influence the great collective powers of evolution and decay.

THE PSYCHOLOGICAL TERMS

The religious viewpoint immediately provides the insight into two opposite human attitudes. The first is the readiness or willingness to discover what God wants us to do; and the second is the lack of this inclination, or even the trick (mostly unconscious) of choosing a philosophy or religious interpretation according to our egocentric desires, and then calling it the will of God. This latter attitude will be described here as idolatry.

Our viewpoint and therefore our terminology, as we shall see, can be described essentially in pairs of opposites. The opposites are, objectively, of equal value, but subjectively, one of them predominates at a given time. Such opposites are youth and maturity, femininity and masculinity, individuality and group life, conscious and unconscious existence. The youth may despise old age, but he carries within himself the symptoms of beginning maturity, and even senility. The old man may scoff at his immature youth, but if he were sensitive enough, he would still feel his youth alive in him, paralleling his maturity. In a similar way, a man shows some conscious or unconscious femininity, and the woman some masculinity. By loving each other they will know themselves more completely and thus be able to live life more fully. But without the hidden femininity of his own mind the man could not have understood and loved the woman, and she could not have become "half of his life."

There is neither good nor bad, nor any difference of value in these opposites. They complete each other and cannot exist without each other. But arbitrarily, time and again, we prefer one and reject the other, disturbing in this way our own inner equilibrium, as well as the equilibrium of group life.

Where men have more rights than women or where individuals are more important than the group, or where the group prevails at the expense of the individual, there the wholeness of life is replaced by a rigid preference for one part. Justice is superseded by partiality, and God is replaced by an idol. We do not know much about God and His will, but we do know that He is loving and just. Therefore, the arbitrary preference for one of two equal opposites seems to be against His will. If an individual deifies this kind of injustice, he worships an idol. A deity, loving one nation or one race to the exclusion of the others, is certainly not God, but an idol. Yet God may give one nation, group or individual a special task at a special time for the benefit of all the others; and to understand this would not be idolatry, but real religion.

All the pairs of opposites which we use in our terminology are psychological. Both counterparts are to be found within our experience, and here the equality of rights and values is always a sign of health, whereas rigid bias represents the beginning of decay. But the two attitudes which we first mentioned, namely, compliance with the will of God, and rebellion against it, do not refer to psychological but to metaphysical realities. Therefore, in this case the balance of opposites is not possible; they exclude each other. Between the servant of God and the rebel against Him we can imagine no mutual understanding or acknowledgment, although the two attitudes may be interwoven in a very subtle manner.

The godless attitude is characterized by (conscious or unconscious) rigid judgments. Man thinks he knows what is good or bad, he prefers one thing and condemns its opposite. He likes money and hates poverty. He longs for health and abhors sickness; but in so doing, in "taking thought" as the New Testament puts it, he disturbs his inner equilibrium, creating exactly what he seeks to avoid: fear, tension, sickness and poverty. The more eagerly a person wants to avoid a mistake, the more he is bound to make it. In other cases the arbitrary judgment of a whole group leads to the condemnation of and enmity against another group. The hatred between feudalism and capitalism, or capitalism and socialism, are historical diseases of this kind; they are idolatry.

What the will of God may be in a given situation has to be found for every moment anew. The general revelations as we find them in the Scriptures allow for opposite interpretations and applications in every case, as religious wars and theological controversies have proved throughout history. Every special application means a new decision and therefore new responsibility, and every new understanding of a given statement means creativeness. The will of

God cannot be figured out in a handbook of morals providing the solution for every problem and the answers to all questions. This would replace creativeness by legality, and the living God by a dead idol. The will of God cannot be expressed in ethics, nor in psychology. Our terminology must refrain from any direct statement about His will.

But indirectly the theologian, the moralist, and the psychologist can explore God by finding what contradicts His will. The attitude which we call rebellion against God, whether it is conscious defiance or unconscious indifference, can be investigated and described. As a matter of fact, we know most of the deviations from the will of God. We have carefully searched the different ways in which man tries to escape his destination. Our negative freedom, our power to ignore God, and the possibility of creating our own illusive vision of the world (where we act as if we were God Himself)—this artificial world of sham values and of real suffering constitutes the central field of our psychology.

Our method, therefore, is to discuss the negative and to presuppose the positive. We call this method "nonic" (from the Latin expression *ars nonica*, an art which describes its object by stating what it is not, *quod non est*). Describing a woman, for instance, as neither old, nor ugly, nor boring, may describe her sufficiently.

All our terms, consequently, indicate either the direct negation of something valuable, like egocentricity (the real center does not function, it is superseded by a sham center called the Ego) or the idol (a faulty godhead, or erroneous highest value). Or they may refer indirectly to the lack of equilibrium which is concomitant with deviation, as, for example, aggression, which should be, but usually is not, balanced by sympathy; or forbearance, which should be, but mostly is not, balanced by fortitude. But we should never forget that, according to the nonic principle, the positive is always to be found at the bottom of the negative. There would be no vice if there were no striving for a better life; no suffering, except on the basis of our longing for happiness; no deviation without the existence of the right way. The bad and the imperfect always presuppose the good and the perfect, just as the creation presupposes the creator.

In a similar way, jurisprudence, medicine, and aesthetics have been nonic arts for many centuries. Nobody knew what justice, health, or beauty actually were, but everybody was aware of injustice, sickness and ugliness. Research in all these cases must start from the negative. The disturbances and deficiencies have to be investigated first. Later it may be possible to define, more or less, their positive background.

In several cases we have the choice between two traditions: for example, with regard to the "layers" or "strata" which are usually described as intermediate steps between the two abstract extremes, spirit and matter. It would have been theoretically more correct to follow the tradition of certain esoteric doctrines which distinguish seven layers; but for the application in practical work it seemed desirable to avoid all superfluous subtleties (true as they are) and to limit ourselves to the simple tools which yield the best results in our practical work. Therefore we preferred the classic tradition, namely, the distinction of three layers: body (physical functions), psyche (emotional functions), and mind (intellectual functions).

But the three traditional activities which correspond to these layers—Willing, Feeling and Thinking—are not as important as the direction of their inner processes. Therefore, we have here introduced four modern terms forming two couples of opposites: Differentiation and Integration, Progression and Regression—all taken from the English philosophy of the last century.

In one case, however, a new idea and a new term had to be introduced: the "unconscious of the future." In addition to the old Jungian distinction between the individual and the collective unconscious, there are two kinds or layers of the unconscious, distinguished by their relation to time.

We have to distinguish between the "unconscious of the past," our racial memory and inheritance, and the "unconscious of the future," containing the infinite pyramid of values, possibilities, and tasks, which, as it were, are lying ahead of us. Exactly spoken of, these values are timeless, but they must be lived in the future. The poet must visualize them, the prophet proclaim them, the individual feel them; yet they can be realized, lived, incorporated, not by single individuals, but only by groups of creative people—they are collective powers. We may call the former the historic, and the latter the timeless, unconscious.

All our terms, however, do not claim to represent the

"last word" or the definite "scientific truth." They are means of orientation similar to a map which the traveller may find useful, or may replace by something better, especially if his own experience exceeds the details of our map. They are tools which the craftsman may apply, but the more his craftsmanship develops, the less he will need them; and if he is a poor craftsman, he will fail anyhow. But then he should not blame our tools.

Part Two

OUTLINE OF A RELIGIOUS
PSYCHOLOGY

I

POWER

I. The Problem of Unconscious Power

Human life needs help, otherwise it may destroy itself. The more resourceful we become and the more we develop the technical means of making life beautiful and happy, the more destructive and bloody grow our moral catastrophes, our crimes, revolutions, and wars. We know more or less how to raise and handle cattle, but we do not know how to deal with ourselves and our fellowmen.

Immense hidden powers seem to lurk in the unconscious depths of even the most common man—indeed, of all people without exception. It is these powers, when put under pressure, that are responsible for all great creative efforts, whether in the form of a new technical invention or a work of art. Some of the most important books in the world's literature have been written in prison. The same forces—in people who are driven to despair—turn men into criminals, are responsible for addictions and obsessions, all kinds of madness, and suicide. Where large groups of people have to face this pressure—as is the case during economic depressions, religious persecutions, class struggles and national wars—there arise, on the one hand, heroes who perform the highest deeds of courage and loyalty, while on the other hand thousands or millions of lives are wantonly destroyed. Such is the origin of powerful empires and world-wide religious movements.

What is the relation between the destructive and the creative power? And what are the conditions which make people either creative or destructive? If we want to help ourselves, our friends, and our governments, we should know more about those hidden powers.

We understand, or think we understand, a large number of human reactions. We usually interpret them as the expressions of hunger or love, self-preservation or race-preservation. The exact meaning of these words may be questionable but we comprehend their implications because we have similar experiences in our own lives. That an individual is afraid of losing money or falling sick, that he enjoys being popular or being successful, is taken for granted. In the last analysis, however, it remains difficult to explain what kind of motive or cause may prompt our reactions, attitudes, and developments. And especially in the case of conflict between self- and race-preservation, we do not understand what makes one of the antagonistic motives or forces prevail.

In our discussion, the blind forces of nature not related to any living form shall be called energies (such as electricity and gravitation). They can be understood and used in terms of cause and effect; no moral values or goals, as far as we can see, are involved. And the "life forces," whether they are motives, instincts, or drives, shall be called "powers," and shall be considered in connection with biological or sociological forms. We have to describe them in terms of means and goals, though their highest ends may remain incomprehensible to the human mind.

As soon as we understand the word "preservation" as related to the present form of life, we have to admit that self- and race-preservation can explain only a certain part of human activities. There are evidently other tendencies, desires, or powers, which force us to create and to believe in new ideas and forms. Almost every century produces new visions of individual life and of society, and every time this happens thousands of people are ready to die for these new values. These creative powers are again related to forms, future forms—and the groups motivated by them are inclined to sacrifice the existence of the individual and even of large parts of the race for the sake of a future society of the Golden Jerusalem beyond space and time.

We see then that, beside the power of self-preservation and race-preservation, we have to acknowledge a strange and daring power of self-development and race-development which may one day compel us to become martyrs for values which we do not yet know.

Moreover, we find frequently in young people and especially primitive "red-blooded" people who are still living close to nature, a peculiar longing for danger, adventure, and if necessary for sacrifice of health and life. It sometimes expresses itself as an exuberant desire to meet with the danger of death. The mountaineer realizes a sharpening of all his senses, and a deeper awareness of his being alive when he embarks on a climb which may prove fatal.

The good hunter prefers to hunt lions rather than rabbits. The healthy boy likes to swim across the roughest waters or to drive a hundred miles an hour. And the healthy girl throws herself, even against her own better judgment, into an impossible love affair.

To most of our psychologists this tendency seems to be so strange and inexplicable that they simply explain it away as deviation, neurosis or criminality. They believe that the striving for security is the basic human instinct. And they cannot see that here, where nature still is "red in tooth and claw," bloodshed and sacrifice are the half-conscious, misunderstood, but all-powerful expressions of a central and creative impulse.

Most of us are Hamlets, now-a-days:

> "Thus conscience does make cowards of us all;
> And thus the native hue of resolution
> Is sicklied o'er with the pale cast of thought,
> And enterprises of great pith and moment
> With this regard their currents turn awry,
> And lose the name of action."

We are afraid of this natural urge for danger and adventure, but we may sometimes, as Hamlet did, enjoy its queer excitement and almost prehistoric atmosphere. It tells us that life is useless, that money, reputation, family are worthless, unless we take our life in our hands at least once and throw it deliberately and consciously at the feet of the gods or the demons, regardless of whether they may bless us or destroy us. It is primitive religion, an unconscious groping of blind people attracted by the light.

England has always had the opportunity of sending her young dare-devils all over the seven seas. From the other European countries the young and the stout of heart used to come to America where they became pioneers, gold-diggers, or gangsters. All of them threw themselves at the feet of the demons, and many of them found God beyond the demons. They probably would not have found Him if they had stayed at home.

This crude longing for deeper experiences is the best part of primitive life; it is the compass pointing to danger and adventure as the shortest way to spend the primitive forces and to reach the higher level of culture. What will happen, however, to this longing, how will this power express itself if improving civilization does not allow conquistadores, pirates, gangsters, and pioneers? How will the untamed nature of red-blooded people behave in a "pale-blooded," so-called Christian society? It will start one revolution after the other, unless we find a better way which leads from nature "red in tooth and claw" through the encounter with sacrifice and danger to inner maturity and real religion.

Our inner, unknown power has to face an adequate outer situation in order to be lived out, experienced, and consciously developed until it reaches a more creative level. The potential hero is looking for the possibility of becoming his best self, and, if his environment prevents him from so developing, his true life is not lived and his hidden talents turn into the negative, driving him around like a madman. Unconsciously he tries to find or to create the fire which can purge him; he forces people to fight him, because nothing else can teach him the truth. The more he has gone astray, the more dangerous and painful must be the outer situation for the fulfillment of his inner life —until finally his "power of darkness" will change into the "power of light."

But what about us—the more pale-blooded people, the good citizens with good consciences and good reputations? We do not know much about those demoniac powers. Are we actually less powerful? Has life withdrawn from us? Are there no demons to lure us into danger and crisis and through suffering into fuller life?

Yes, we harbor the same powers in a more subtle form, but not less dangerous and not less helpful. Only it takes more psychology, indeed depth-psychology in the true sense of the word, to explore the unconscious capacities, to unmask them, to lead them and to change them into creativeness. We are more at the mercy of the dark powers than we know. Every one, even the coolest and calmest moralist, is their slave. And to master consciously our unconscious forces is the only way which can help us to replace our bloody so-called civilization by real culture.

2. Individual Unconscious Power

There are many signs indicating to each of us that our unconscious power is waiting for release. Even trivial incidents betray its pressure. A person is in a hurry to get to a movie; impatiently he buttons his coat and one of the buttons flies off. His reaction is anger. With a furious kick he sends the rebellious button under the couch and then spends ten minutes trying to get it back. The more he hurries, the more excited he gets, and the more he delays his departure by giving vent to his excitement. This reaction may be comprehensible to most of us. We would feel a similar impulse, but at the same time we deem it ridiculous, uncontrolled, and inadequate. A mature person does not behave in this way. But the willful and impatient impulse scoffs at our maturity.

Words like "primitive," "childish," "immature" shed some light on the pattern of such a reaction. But they give no explanation of the source and nature of the explosive power which is involved. We may only guess that its destructive form is not the genuine one. Originally, haste may have been the proper reaction to pressure of time; here, however, it leads to blunders (tearing off the button), creates delay and greater hurry and further blunders. The power which produces the "haste" seems to have a history and a development which branches either towards the good or the bad. Yet we are unaware of it, it remains unconscious, until its results confront us with disaster.

Imagine that some one tells a story at your expense. You may laugh and simply consider it out of place. At another time you may resent it, but answer it with a better and more ingenious joke, thus defeating the aggressor. In a third case, you may feel deeply hurt and be unable to control yourself. Sometimes such a joke may work like a spark which is dropped into a barrel of gunpowder. A terrific explosion may be released by a small stimulus. This power is evidently stored in our unconscious mind. Its release can be postponed and led into different channels. The good answer, the creative joke, or a destructive fight may be the result. By whom, how, and with the help of what other force can this power be controlled?

Nobody likes rats, mice or bugs. Some people resent them so much that they find their presence literally unbearable. One day, so the story goes, a large meeting of belligerent suffragettes in London could not be controlled by the authorities. The policemen were scared to death by the shouting and gesticulating ladies. One of them, however, was a wise man. He released a mouse in the midst of the women and three minutes later the meeting place was empty. Who can explain the power of the mouse? Who knows its origin? It seems a demoniac power.

Sigmund Freud has pointed out that some of our blunders, such as slips of the tongue, and at least part of our forgetfulness are due to unconscious tendencies which conflict with our conscious intentions. For example, a woman who is very anxious to have children always reads the word "stock" as "stork." That happens against her conscious will, and is caused by the deeper instinct which controls her reactions more than she knows. Innumerable examples of this kind have been analyzed during the last fifty years.

Then there are the strong tendencies which support our so-called bad habits. If a person unconsciously toys with a spoon when he sits at the table or "doodles" when listening to a lecture he may try very hard to overcome this habit. He probably will not be able to do so. Careful analysis usually shows that these are not casual happenings. Bad habits frequently express unconscious tendencies which cannot be mastered or suppressed. They have to be accepted, assimilated, and developed into something better. Otherwise they will continue to disturb the individual.

Similar to the bad habits are the cravings and addictions like alcoholism and gambling. They often turn out to be substitutes for improperly used or unused possibilities of life. The born artist, if he does not know that he is an artist or does not allow himself to be creative, may become a drunkard or a gambler. And the same is true with regard to sexual passions and perversions. They also represent the "unlived life." The unknown power is led into the wrong channels. It becomes destructive and finally may result in neurotic diseases or crimes. Life, as it were, has entrusted us with great capacities. If we misuse them they turn against us and destroy us and themselves.

Here we are confronted with an important theoretical problem. It is indeed the problem on the solution of which depends our practical mastery of unconscious power, and therefore the failure or success of human development. It is the question: What is the relationship between ourselves and our "power"? What do we mean when we say, for example, "I do not want to smoke, but my urge or craving or vice is stronger than I am, and so I smoke against my will"? Who is "I," and what is "it" which is stronger than I? Am "I" part of "it" or is "it" part of myself? Or are both "it" and "I" separate "entities" of equal standing?

The popular answer to this decisive question is usually given in terms of Freudian psychoanalysis: "I" is my conscious personality; "it" is the unconscious energy (libido) which is cut off (repressed) from consciousness.

For a beginning this crude application of Freudianism may be sufficient. It gives us a vague idea that there is a conflict within our psychic life and that unification or integration would be the way out. Yet a more careful investigation reveals very soon that we need a better description. What we call "it"—the powers, instincts, tendencies we have to deal with—is not completely unknown and in most cases certainly not unconscious during the time that "it" controls us. The smoker who does not want to smoke is aware of his vice. He may even understand its meaning, origin, and final goal. And still it is stronger than what he calls "I."

On the other hand, this "I" is not entirely conscious. It is known only to a certain extent and its "shadow-side," the less agreeable qualities (for example, greediness, envy, irritability) may be excluded from consciousness just as the "unlived life" which expresses itself in the addiction to the cigarette. The demarcation line between the unconscious and the conscious does not coincide with the border between our "I" and the powers which we want to explore. Further investigation is needed.

A taxi-driver had a quarrel with his colleague. Later when he was asked by the judge why he had hurt his friend, he said, "He accused me wrongly, and then my Irish got me—one of my grandparents was Irish—and so I just let him have it with my fists." The taxi-driver's explanation in terms of inheritance may be completely wrong, but it indicates that he is aware of his temperamental pattern. Sometimes he may try to master it, but sometimes he allows it to run away with him. Then he is identified with "it." He is then, as it were, completely Irish, and he may say, "I am like my grandfather—I will kill you!" In this moment the word "I" denotes his fury, and his other qualities and attitudes which prevail at other times now are superseded. They are overruled like the minority in Congress and have to wait until the party in power collapses—the relationship between "I" and "it" is unstable.

3. COLLECTIVE UNCONSCIOUS POWER

The next step in our investigation seems to add a new difficulty. Both the "I" and the "it" can be found as expressions of group life as well as of individual life. "I" then is replaced by "We," yet the instinctive power remains the same, its nature becoming more evident. Finally this new aspect of the problem will lead us to decisive discoveries.

A teacher arouses the patriotism of her class. The waves of enthusiasm are running high, and she is proud of her achievement. "Everyone must be ready to die for his country!" The boys are excited: "To hell with the cowards!—Let's kill the enemy!" They yell and scream. "Hurrah!—There he is!—Get him!" The teacher becomes afraid. She shouts, "Order! Quiet! You cannot serve your country without discipline!" But hell is loose already and her angry voice stirs the fire like a pair of bellows. The boys jump on the desks and an inkpot flies against the wall. "Hurrah!"

The cry for discipline, the anger of offended authority on the part of the teacher, and the patriotic courage turning into riot on the side of the students—both are different channels for the same power. The waters of a river are divided by an island. Behind the island they meet again now coming from opposite directions, and they clash like inimical forces. The striving for discipline and the striving for unbounded expression of energy are in the last analysis the same river which contradicts itself.

Both the teacher and the students identify themselves with their respective emotional attitudes. The teacher says: "My anger is justified. I *must* be angry. If only I could express my feelings more adequately the boys would understand and obey." And the students say: "It is fun to feel as excited as this; and even if we were to try to stop ourselves, we couldn't do it." Here we find some kind of collective personality. The students would not say, "I am excited" but "We are excited." The collective power has submerged, at least for the time being, their different individualities.

This phenomenon leads us into the problems of group-psychology and mass-psychology. And we have to solve these problems if we want to understand history; and we have to master these collective powers if we want to control the development of the future. The next step, however, on the way to this almost superhuman goal has to be a simple investigation of facts. We have to explore the points which the psychology of primitive tribes and the psychology of our own unconscious have in common. This will shed new light on the intricate problems of the collective power.

A primitive tribe can be excited to collective emotions

such as fear or hatred or joy. The cause may be an outer reality like thunderstorms, eclipses, wild beasts, enemies, or visitors. Or it may be the inner readiness and expectation of the community aroused by religious ceremonies or magic achievements. The reaction is the emotional discharge of a super-individual power. The individual cannot refrain from participating in this experience. And the proper description is not that the individual has or realizes the excitement, but rather that the emotional excitement seizes and obsesses the individual.

Later the same people may find themselves in quite a different mood. They may have gone through utmost fear and despair yesterday. And today after a magic performance of their medicine-men they may be filled with courage and confidence. Looking back and trying in their own mind to understand the change, they may ascribe the fear and the courage to the presence of super-individual entities. Demons, spirits, gods can animate and support the tribe or forsake it, blind it, and lead it into annihilation.

The medicine-man who propitiates the spirit of war and exorcises the demon of fear or—even better—sends the demon of fear into the enemy's camp, can master the fate of the tribe almost as an artist masters his clay. And there is not much difference between the medicine-man of ten thousand years ago and the political propagandizer of our time. We call the demons and gods by other names, confusing them with other facts, speaking of patriotism or duty or war-hysteria or mass-phobia. The instinctive power is still the same. And even the mysterious test of its presence, well-known to modern psychology, does not change.

Three men spellbound by a super-individual spirit can achieve much more than these same men could do under separate impulse with their strength simply added together. The group is more than the sum-total of its members. Where does this additional power come from? The demons are still alive, and they are nearer to us than we usually admit.

The most important of all of them is the great and bloody god, Mars. He was in disfavor for a long time. The poets ridiculed him and the scientists explained him away. The causes of war were supposed to be economic interests, the need of markets, or of raw materials, or the class struggle, or the ambition of the generals. But then the god shook his head, the nations clashed, and the scientists admitted that all the explanations they could think of did not fully account for the slaughter. It seemed evident that nobody wanted the war but that it had happened nevertheless. Our fear, it is said, creates what we want to avoid. This is the pattern of our neuroses. But if wars are neuroses of mankind, we have to investigate the power that prompts them all the more. And this power, until we find a better name for it, may be called Mars.

The name does not matter. Instead of Mars we could say just as well Ares, Thor, Vishnu, or even Lord Sabaoth, the Lord of Hosts. But looking at this row of gods or demons of war, we discover another fact, namely the indistinctness, cloudiness, and plasticity of the collective powers. The biological basis is always the same. The readiness to fight seems to be a general human quality, though different races share it in different part. The outer forms, however, differ according to technical means and moral standards. The bushman with his club, the mediæval knight with his splendid armor, the modern parachutist with his elaborate equipment—all of them are inspired by the same collective power, or they will fail. All of them are courageous but the style of their courage and the goal of their exploits differ. They may be more bloodthirsty or more magnanimous, more daring or more cautious, more ingenious or more stubborn. In spite of all these differences they are psychologically—at least in the moment of combat—in a similar situation. Their "I" is more or less replaced by "We," and this "We" is identified with the power which we call Mars.

Here we have to deal with collective powers which master the style of life in groups, movements, social classes, and nations. They are like enormous billows coming up from the depth of the ocean. Our private instincts, convictions, ideals, and fears then represent small waves and shallow cross-currents which may influence the surface of the water only for a short time. The "man in the street" who constitutes "the mass" has little or no "private waves." He is controlled by the huge billows of the herd instinct. The individualist consciously holds private opinions and inclinations which may contradict the herd instinct, although unconsciously he may still be moved by the collective powers. The so-called great men and the leaders of mankind are those whose individual wave is in accordance with the rising tide. They do consciously what the mass, because of their lack of consciousness, can never achieve. They solve the problems of their century and their success changes our civilization. Such were Saint Francis and Luther, Washington and Lincoln, Shakespeare and Goethe.

The greatest historical events, however, have always appeared as startling cases of insanity or crime to most of the reasonable onlookers, the rising tide of the ocean being then in discord with the individual waves as well as the big billows. Alexander the Great was a powerful criminal, an aggressor, and conqueror without legal rights; but he plucked a fruit which was ripened by history. And all his predecessors and successors, all the Nebuchadnezzars and Cæsars, did the same. Jesus of Nazareth, on the other hand, was deemed to be an obsessed fool, and even nowadays some people think of him as a paranoiac. And it was the same with Buddha and Lao-tse before him. But Jesus was the turning point of the tide. The flood now rises in spite of all the waves and billows. There was no room for a second one like him. The Cæsars condemned him but he did not condemn them. He is still waiting for them.

The terrific red-blooded power that inspired Alexander's legions to sacrifice their lives on the battlefield, and the other power, the shining love which filled the Christian martyrs with joy when they were torn by beasts in the Roman arena, these two powers shake and illuminate our own world even now. And they seem to be as young and dynamic as they have ever been. We must study them, understand them, deal with them; indeed we must choose between them or we shall be lost in the chaos.

II

E G O

1. The Problem of the Self

Our problem is rather involved. We have mentioned the fact that the psychic power is always related to form. Development, change, destruction or preservation of special living forms is always intended. A second observation, previously mentioned, must be recalled here—namely, that this power cannot be understood in terms of cause and effect. Causality can explain only an unspecific kind of destruction—a falling stone may cause the death of a person. But growth and development imply more. The Tea Party in Boston, in addition to many other "causes," prompted the War of the Revolution. But this result was not the unavoidable effect in the sense of a natural law or mathematical necessity. It was a creative reaction of individuals and groups who were inspired by a growing vision of a growing future. Human life has to be understood in terms of means and goals.

But the highest goal remains unknown; it is an infinite value. We think of the goals not in the sense of rigid, mechanical forces determining the means (this again would exclude freedom, responsibility, and creativeness).

We think of the goals of life as values which may or may not be reached, which can be interchanged or replaced, and which build an infinite pyramid pointing to the unknown highest value which is the purpose of creation and the will of God.

Here many questions arise which cannot be discussed in this book. Only some of them may be mentioned. What is the relation between the powers we are talking about and those infinite values? Are they identical or opposite? Are they dependent on or independent of each other? Are all the destructive powers derived from constructive ones as it has been suggested with regard to obsessions and addictions? How many powers are there? Are they creating or created (*natura naturans,* or *natura naturata*)? And last but not least, is there one Creator, God, to be assumed behind all this mysterious life? Is it unavoidable to assume His existence? And if so what do we know about Him? What is His Will with regard to us? And how can we do His will if we are controlled by those super-individual powers which we do not know?

The last question is the basis of the present book. How can we do or even find the will of God if we are largely controlled by unknown unconscious powers which may cause us to do what we do not want to do? But before we can try to answer this question we have still to ask another question. Who is "we"? What about our consciousness? Are we, the conscious individuals who ask and answer, identical with the psychic powers we try to explore? Or are we identical with the values and goals of development? Or are we something different? Who are we?—Or, using the formula of the foregoing chapter: what does the individual mean when he says "I"?

The problem of the human "I" cannot be separated from the problem of consciousness though, as we have said, consciousness and "I" are not identical. You cannot say "I" without being conscious, but you can be conscious without being completely yourself. You can honestly say, "I am not I in this moment." An artist in the depressed state of mind which often occurs in the interval between two creative achievements may be clearly conscious of his momentary impotence and shallowness. He suffers because he is conscious of his not being himself, that is, of not being creative. What he calls his real Self is, as it were, not awake; it exists, but temporarily it does not work.— Our consciousness is changing every hour. It can be clear or dim, rich or poor, dynamic or static. What we call our Self, however, seems to be there as long as we live. It does not cease even when we sleep. Sometimes it is creative and sometimes it hides itself. We do not feel it then, but it is there.

What we mean by the word "I" in a given moment may be very different—and has to be distinguished psychologically—from what we mean in the next moment when we say "I myself as I really am." The temporary "I" looks at the deeper and more essential "I myself" much as "I" looks at the emotional power which it remembers from yesterday. Or with regard to consciousness some one may say: "I am conscious of the fact that I am dull and sleepy today, but I know that I could be wide awake, courageous, and creative. If my real Self would awake to consciousness I would be different from what I am now."

The human mind is accustomed to seeing—and indeed wants to see—definite forms. Therefore it remembers the collective powers in the form of images and very soon ascribes to them the dignity of independent entities. The images become "objects" and are believed to move around in space and time. In this sense the patriotic enthusiasm of the home-front or the super-individual fury of the battlefield are seen as a collective spirit which seizes the individual minds; and soon it is symbolized as a super-human figure, and, by a primitive mind, idolized as a god or a demon. In a similar way our own remembrances and ideas about our own "real Self" are seen as an image. And very soon this image becomes an "objective reality." What we think of ourselves becomes more important than what we really are (because we know the images of ourselves, but we do not know what our "Selves" really are).

Thus we may say: "I cannot concentrate on a book when there is noise. I need perfect calm. This is one of my innate peculiarities. It is a quality of my real Self." How can we know whether this is a quality of our deepest "Self" or of our temporary "I"? For thousands of years men have taken it for granted that we have to hate our enemies. This seemed to be the most natural reaction of every human Self. Then the man from Nazareth taught us that it is possible to love our enemies. And now more and more people are discovering that the closer they come to their real Selves the more it is impossible for them to hate their enemies. They change when the Self emerges;

they look at the world with different eyes; they act differently; and the world reacts differently too. Reality changes.*

The real Self, now, seems to be a goal of development rather than an immediate experience. It may be the channel through which the infinite highest value draws us towards the top of the pyramid of means and goals. But then it is infinite itself, and cannot be pictured as a definite image. It is not possible to have an adequate image of our real Self—just as it is impossible to have such an image of God. We are infinite like Him, and increasingly so the more we are aware of our real Selves.

Our ideas, therefore, concerning the inherent qualities and conditions of the human Self are necessarily incomplete. And we have to discriminate between the image of the Self and the real Self. We call the former the Ego, and describe it as the sum total of what we know or what we think we know about ourselves. The Ego is a system of statements concerning our goals and means, gifts, capacities and limitations—statements such as: "I would be a good musician if my parents had given me the proper education." "I will become famous, rich, or morally good

* The same person, having gone through the amazing experience which changed his hatred into love, may find himself furiously fighting again. Now he fights his former enemies, knowing that he loves them and that he has to change them in order to help them. Thus Jesus fought the Pharisees and the Sadducees, relentlessly and undauntedly. The creative fury of such a fight is the exact opposite of hatred. A fighter who hates is a poor marksman; his emotion blinds him. The sacred fury of creative men is the same in the artist's study, on the speaker's platform, and on the battlefield. This fury, originating from the very center of mankind, provides unlimited resourcefulness, endurance, creativity and often clairvoyance.

if only I can get rid of my present handicap." "I am a loyal friend, but when my friends laugh at me I feel like hitting them."

The Ego-image is the part or aspect of our real Self which has become conscious in earlier years. It may have been partly forgotten again; it has usually been misunderstood; and worst of all it is considered to be a stable object which can be described like a house or a tree—while actually the Self is indescribable, impenetrable and inaccessible to our research.

In the vague manner of popular philosophy we may call this Self the source of our most creative and most vital actions, the core of human personality; or, following the unanimous tradition of the mystics: the inner light, the soul's deepest ground, the empty center of the inner universe;—but we only realize the more vividly that we do not know its true nature.

The psychological statements which we can make so far about the real Self are not so much the result of scientific observation as the result of philosophical thought and religious experience. They are more negative, stating what the Self is not, than positive, defining what it is. It is important, however, for our later discussions, to explain carefully what we think about this mysterious center of the human personality.

The Self (in the sense in which we use the word here) seems to be essential to human life. In animal life its presence is questionable. We don't know whether a dog has a Self. But we are enticed to ascribe a certain kind of Selfhood to a *community* of ants or bees rather than to the individual insect. And the same is true with regard to primitive men and little children. They seem to have merely a "tribal consciousness," and their Self, the source of their strength, and the center of their impetus, belongs to the group and not to the individual.

The Self is invisible, just as consciousness and life itself are invisible. We know them only from our own *inner* experience. Or we infer them from outer results. The Self can never be made an object. If we try to explore it, it escapes. If we handle it, as we handle dead things, it eludes us. If we formulate its qualities, and the laws of its reactions, it suddenly shows different attitudes and behaves in a way which could by no means have been predicted. It is incalculable and free because of its creativeness. Here the "nonic method" is the only adequate approach.

The Self exists and works in time but it cannot be located in space. It certainly is connected with the body as long as the body is alive. But it has no special organ as its residence. Its efficacy depends on the inner glands as much as on the central nervous system, and on blood and blood circulation as much as on the solar plexus. Yet in spite of all this it acts independently, using the body and its glands and nerves creatively, as a strategist uses his army. Like him it is limited by the deficiencies of the instrument; but like him it can achieve the most astonishing results with weakened forces in a stroke of unexpected ingenuity.

What we know about this enigmatical Self we owe to the fact that it frequently contradicts the instinctive powers which constitute our unconscious life. In every man's life, as we have pointed out, there is a time when he may say,

"If I am myself, I want to do this; but sometimes my emotions get the better of me and then I find myself doing just the opposite." This conflict therefore will be the starting point for our further investigations.

Our religious ideas about the human Self have a better basis in real experience than the philosophical statements. Religiously we may say we can realize that our true Self is more than our conscious personality. The more a person finds himself, the more he discovers that his personal interest is replaced by his responsibility for the whole. He is really himself only as far as he is a member of his group; and his group is alive only as far as it is related to mankind. The real Self therefore is not "I"; it is "We."

Moreover, the human Self is not only human love and brotherhood; it is at the same time the creativity of the Creator, working through human individuals. He who really finds himself finds God. And he may say, as Saint Paul did, "It is no longer I who live; Christ lives in me." —In this sense our true Self is the final goal of our religious development. At first it is "I"; then it becomes "We"; and at last it will be "He."

2. THE SHAM-CENTER: THE EGO

However carefully we may look at ourselves, we can never discover what we really are. We may discover some of our present qualities, and putting them together with remembrances of earlier experiences we may achieve a self-portrait which bears some similarity to our real Self. Our desires and fears, however, will distort the picture, in addition to the fact that always the larger part of our life remains unconscious. This inadequate self-portrait, this image or symbol of our real Self, is what we call our Ego.

There would be no need to take this Ego-image seriously and to give it a special name if it remained just an image, an idea, developing when we develop, and changing when its model, the real Self, changes. But the Ego tends to lead a life of its own. It remains, as we have said, an independent, rigid "object," while the Self changes, or more exactly speaking, displays new qualities and growing maturity. In many cases the Self and the Ego develop in opposite directions.

A person may have quite an optimistic Ego. "With me everything is all right—nothing bad can happen to me." Yet his real Self may grow more and more desperate. He does not really believe in the egocentric mask that he wears, but he is able for a long time to deceive himself and his friends. Here the conscious personality is centered around the optimistic Ego-image; the truth, the desperation of the Self, remains unconscious until the mask breaks down and the truth comes to light.

Even this self-deception would not be too serious a mistake and would not last long if our actions and decisions were controlled by the original center and source of our life: the real Self. Yet, as soon as our consciousness is dominated by the Ego-image, our behavior-pattern and our new decisions become "egocentric." They serve the Ego instead of the Self. They apparently originate in the Ego, and are shaped by the Ego's vision of life (for example, the crude optimism mentioned above). This is what

we call egocentricity. The opposite attitude is characterized
by the fact that actions and reactions flow from the real
center and are shaped by the creative instincts and intui-
tions which surround the real Self and serve as its genuine
channels of expression. We describe this attitude as creativity, and we assume that egocentricity, in spite of a certain resourcefulness, will always remain barren and uncreative.

Suppose you want to write an important letter to the
board of directors of a large organization. Your Ego demands that you make a good impression, not hurting the
feelings of Mr. A, nor contradicting the convictions of
Mrs. B. And here you sit writing out six different drafts
and rejecting them all. Your ambitious egocentric goals
are not yet satisfied, nor your subtle egocentric fears ap-
peased. You try again; but now you are tense, you get
excited, and you fail even more than before. The Self
would write the letter easily, honestly, courageously and
successfully. But the Ego does not allow this. As long as
the Ego-pattern is the basis of our activity we are bound
to fail, sooner or later. The Ego is helpless, rigid and shallow as compared with the inexhaustible creativity of the
Self.

The collective powers are to be found on the side of the
Self; while the strength which is available to the Ego is
limited to shrewd cunning and sentimental excitement,
cleverly used, but not at all creative. Where an egocentric
person explodes in fury and rage he already comes close
to the collapse of the Ego. The power of his outburst is
already due to collective powers which may get the better

of him very soon. He still uses his fury for the sake of his Ego, but already he feels insecure in his own house, and the more insecure he feels the more furious he becomes.

Our Ego, therefore, has to defend itself not only against outer enemies, competitors and exploiters, but also against inner dangers such as emotions, desires and thoughts which would destroy the Ego-pattern from within. Where the Ego-pattern says, "I am a good boy, I stay at home," there the desire to explore the world, to have all sorts of adventure, and to face all kinds of danger—a healthy boy's desire for self-development—has to be discounted, fought off, and finally repressed into the unconscious. On the other hand, if the Ego-pattern prescribes being a bad boy, breaking windowpanes, doing mischief and never telling the truth, then all inclinations towards honesty, loyalty and kindness have to be repressed.*

Thus a large part of our functioning and of our inherited collective powers remains unconscious, under-developed and primitive, because those activities would conflict with our egocentric pattern of life. The Ego is not only the insincere mask which overlays the real Self; it is also the censor and appraiser who casts aside into the unconscious or admits into consciousness our inner impulses, creative thoughts, and emotional reactions.

The Ego is the factor which determines our outer fate and our inner development more decisively than any other factor in life. And its influence as we shall see is always

---

* The relationship between the three factors, the Self, the Ego, and the repressed "powers" can be better understood by comparing Diagrams I and II (pages 264 and 267) and the corresponding descriptions.

unfavorable. The study of the Ego is therefore as important as the study of the collective powers. In fact we cannot understand one without understanding the other. The Ego keeps the powers unconscious, and the powers, threatening to destroy the Ego, force it to defend itself with all its shrewdness and cunning. The solution of this inner conflict would free the imprisoned powers, lead them from negative to positive expression, and replace the Ego by the real Self—the goal of our religious endeavor for centuries.

The investigation of egocentricity has been one of the main objectives of depth-psychology for as long as this psychology has existed. We know how egocentricity begins in the life of the individual. We do not know, however, how it began in the life of mankind. We have sufficient evidence for the statement that the new-born child is not egocentric. The baby is as trustful and as responsive as the members of primitive tribes—though the individualistic psychologists of the last generation cannot believe it. Egocentricity is not innate nor inherent in human nature; but it can easily be induced by outer influences.

Egocentricity begins in early childhood as a natural adjustment to the child's egocentric environment. It is a normal reaction to an abnormal situation—the abnormal situation being the average situation. The abnormality of the child's environment may be described generally as the absence of the right kind of love. This abnormality carries over from one generation to the next.

We certainly love our children. Our love, however, is egocentric and therefore incomplete. It either lacks wisdom—we pamper our children; or it lacks warmth—we are too strict and too demanding. And where exceptional parents happen to be more or less mature and able to avoid those two mistakes, other educators come in and teach the children the erroneous lesson of our civilization, that only egocentricity enables them to live.

Many parents are convinced that the child compelled to live in an egocentric world must first of all learn to defend himself. And this self-defense they can only imagine as an egocentric attitude. They teach their children egocentricity on purpose. "You must beat your competitors! Be smart! Be at the top of the class! Excel in popularity!" These are the semi-Christians who think that the Sermon on the Mount holds good only on Sunday, but that during the week we must kill or be killed.

Every generation, not so much by words as by actions, forces the next generation to become even more egocentric. This unintentional teaching is a fiendish process. It affects the very center of children's lives. And it is much more successful than any other educational endeavor. We more or less destroy the creativity and happiness of those whom we love most; yet we have a good conscience because "we do our best," and we simply cannot believe that we participate in the common human fate of transmitting our own deficiencies and weaknesses to the next generation. We may admit that our parents did this to us, but we cannot think that we do it to our children.

3. TRANSMISSION OF EGOCENTRICITY

We talk rather glibly about the deviation and the guilt of humanity. But here where a large part of our own guilt may become visible we prefer to say that all children are born as egocentric individualists and that we try to soften their *"hard-boiled egos."* The truth is the opposite: they are born soft and responsive, and we change them into hard-boiled egos by our own egocentricity. Yet guilty in this case is not just one father or one mother or some teachers; guilty is our whole generation, and the former generation also. Our private guilt is part of our collective guilt, and we have to pay the penalties as collective debtors.

Our children appear on this earth, as far as we can see, in a state of actual innocence, neither good nor bad in themselves, and equally ready to develop good and bad qualities, according to circumstances. During the first period of their lives they are so completely a part of the higher unit, the group, that they express like mirrors the emotional situation of their environment. In a nursery, if one baby cries, all cry; if one laughs, all do the same. If the mother worries, the child is depressed; and where the parents fight with each other (even without betraying consciously any sign of their conflict) the children are inwardly disturbed and insecure.

This important fact, which adds so greatly to our parental responsibility, was first discovered among primitive tribes. If one of his fellow-tribesmen is hurt or offended, a bushman will feel it. Whatever happens, happens to the tribe and not to the individual. All experiences and reactions seem to be more or less collective. The individual has not yet emerged out of the tribe. Consciousness is still a tribal and not yet an individual quality. The group feels, thinks, and wills; the individual, as separated from the others, is dull and callous. "We" has not yet become differentiated into "I" and "You."

The French ethnographer, Lucien Levy-Bruhl, has carefully investigated these facts, terming them "participation mystique." We find the same attitude in all our babies, and we cannot see any mystery in it. They behave like little savages, it is true; they are organs of a higher organism, the family, like tribesmen; they are loyal, and at the same time unreliable, wise and stupid, creative and narrowly limited—and therefore bound to go astray, unless they are led by better leaders than we are.

We call their inner attitude the "original We-feeling," and we assume that it arises from their real creative Self which still coincides with the real Self of the group. The small child is not yet conscious of his center; but he is closer to the real Self and therefore to real love and creativity than any other member of the group. The adults are conscious of their centers—but they have exchanged the group center (the Self) for the individual center (the Ego). Therefore they have to become like children again, discovering anew that their real center is the group and behind the group the whole, and finally God. And they should go this way, back into childhood, without forgetting their adult consciousness and their individual responsibility. Then, out of the child's "original We-feeling" and the adult's "individual consciousness" will arise the "creative We-experience" of the mature and fully responsible personality.

The We-feeling of the new-born baby is potentially

complete, but it is plastic and weak. It immediately mirrors, as we have said, the warmth or the lack of warmth and the wisdom or the lack of wisdom, of its environment. The child lives out of the real center, yet in a very primitive way. It needs help, it needs the real We-group; yet the family is a sham We-group, a group perhaps with 40% genuine We-feeling and 60% egocentricity. In the family the real Self has been replaced by an association of Egos with limited liabilities. And the newest member of this association has to accept the conditions of membership. The child therefore either has to give up its spontaneity, its original Self, and a large part of its collective power, or it has to give up its membership in the group. Anticipating later results we may say that the child has to choose unconsciously between God and the family, since the family is alienated from God. And the child always chooses the family, and that means egocentricity. The reason for this empirical fact is very simple.

The child cannot yet distinguish between the parents and God. To him the parents are God. The love for man and the love for God are identical. Subjectively the child does not realize that there is a choice. He accepts his parents as they are and applies what he learns from them to life and mankind and God. They are his encyclopædic knowledge of religion.

Here is the point where religious education begins. If we destroy the early We-feeling of our children, we destroy the basis of their religious faith. If we are bad parents, the child learns that God is bad.

Many psychologists tell us that monotheistic religion

is "nothing but" the projection of the father-image into the universe. This is true in many cases but only as far as the poor pedagogy of egocentric parents distorts the children's imagery, represses the collective powers, and replaces their creative Self by fearful and powerless Egos. The parents exchange within the children "the glory of the immortal God for the semblance of the likeness of mortal man" (Romans 1:23). Later we shall see how God and his creative powers destroy the wrong religious ideas and finally replace them by truth.

Here are two drastic examples showing how egocentricity is transferred from one generation to the other and how the wrong conception of God is an integral part of the wrong vision of life.

In the first example the father, a successful business man, pretends to be a very good Christian. This, however, does not prevent him from unscrupulous competition in business and reckless tyranny in his home. His wife and his three sons tremble at his rage. Nobody dares to oppose his wishes and whims. The family goes to church twice every Sunday. The two older boys very soon learn to say "yes" and to do "no." They read funny stories during the sermon and the second boy develops an admirable talent as a cartoonist, drawing caricatures of all the pious people in the church. These two sons were alienated from Christianity for almost a lifetime. They assume that a cause supported by this kind of a paternal tyrant cannot be a good cause.

The mother and the youngest son are of a softer constitution. They take religion seriously; they are startled when the father shouts that according to Scriptures disobedient children will burn in everlasting fire. They try to be obedient but it is impossible. The father tells them to wear new clothes, but to spend no money. They have to cheat him, and that means to cheat God.

For them the image of God is characterized by the same features as the father. He is a furious and revengeful God, jealous of his rights, and inexorable in his judgment. When they read the Bible, which they do constantly, they always find this picture of the thundering Jehovah. They are not able to see any kindness in his character. The word "forgiveness" is empty and meaningless and the expression "our Father in heaven" means simply "our terrible judge who knows our guilt."

The youngest son had to go through a painful religious crisis of several years before he—at least partly—overcame his wrong ideas about God. Whether his brothers and his mother have ever found the way out is not known.

In the second case, both parents were lenient, weak and mild. They brought up their two children, a boy and a girl, without any harshness, discipline, or constraint. This was their interpretation of love. They believed that it was not necessary to struggle and to toil since God gives to his children what they need. Their understanding of non-resistance to evil was: if the boy at the age of five climbed on his father's desk and stepped on the letters and the books, and spilled the ink, the father had to take it as sent from the Lord. He should try to rejoice in it and he certainly must not punish the child.

Other people, however, had different ideas about education. In kindergarten and Sunday School the children behaved as they did at home, but they met with disaster, and the catastrophe was the more terrible because it was entirely unexpected. The only explanation was: "These are bad people; we and our parents are good. We serve God; the others outside our family serve the Devil." Their God became a tribal God, a family protector, as in the most primitive religion.

The parents allowed them everything and gave them all they wanted. And the parents received everything from the family God. This God seemed to be a kind of department store where the good family had infinite credit— until one day the father lost his job and a few weeks later the mother fell ill. Not being accustomed to any disappointment they found the darkness so black that it was incompatible with the existence of any God. The family God had failed. It was a crisis of utmost severity. Finally they decided that there was no God at all, and the government with its WPA had to take care of them.

In both cases, the original "We" had been destroyed very early. In the first case, the children learned that there was a group of good people represented and headed by the infallible father but that they themselves, being bad, did not belong to this group. Therefore they developed a strong feeling of inferiority and guilt. In the second case, the children learned that they were good people themselves and that the world was bad. Therefore they developed a feeling of moral superiority. Later, however, they discovered that the good group grew smaller and weaker; and finally God Himself proved to be on the side of the bad people—if He existed at all. The children felt forsaken and utterly helpless. In spite of all their righteous pretensions, their moral superiority was no defense against the feeling of utmost insecurity.

In both cases, the "good group" exists only subjectively in the children's imagination. Objectively, it is a "sham-We group," an egocentric group with a moral façade. In the first case, this group is destroyed from inside by the tyranny of the father. In the second case, it breaks down under pressure from outside. The group of righteous children of God cannot protect its members and God Himself evidently does not desire that they be protected.

The result is the same in all cases. The child is finally left without the support of any group. Loneliness, the necessity of self-defense, the unending fight against deceitful enemies, and the distrust of unreliable friends, are the outstanding features in all the different forms of egocentricity. And worst of all, the child has already sacrificed a large part of his capacities, and in most cases has renounced the very source of his creativity, his real Self, before the struggle began. So, he has to defend himself without adequate preparation.

He has lived for some time in a "sham-We group," namely in his family, against his original nature. He was not allowed to develop his collective powers. His creativity was not wanted. In our first case, the father did not tolerate the children's creative ideas. In the second case, all sound development would have had to surmount the narrow limits of the family; but the outer world was too dangerous; safety was preferable to creativity.

More generally we may say that in both these cases the hard task of the growing human mind, the journey from original We-experience, through loneliness and individuation to the mature wisdom of a conscious We-group, was imposed on the children too early and too suddenly because of the deficiencies of their parents. Thus, the parental egocentricity is handed down to the next generation. Its outer form may vary; sometimes in the succeeding generation it assumes an opposite shape (the son of a miser becomes a spendthrift, and *vice versa*). Yet the degree of deviation remains the same, or is increased: God "avenges the sins of fathers on their children and their children's children, down to the third and fourth generation" (Exodus 34:7, Moffatt).

Moreover, the very essence of "sin" becomes evident. It is the substitution of a sham center, the Ego, for our real center, the Self. And that means three things:

1. Our genuine membership in the group—or the sense of love and brotherhood—is replaced by loneliness, callousness and distrust, the Self being the identical gravitation point of both the group and the individual.

2. Our positive relation to God is replaced by the self-sufficiency of our Ego. We do not know Him any more, and where we still acknowledge His existence intellectually we try to exploit Him in the service of our Ego. (For example, by egocentric prayers.)

3. The subjective experience which results from this double deviation is anxiety. We find anxiety—conscious or unconscious—at the bottom of all egocentricity. Anxiety results from the fact that we are cut off from our creative

center, the Self, and thereby cut off from God as well as from our fellow-men. This center still exists; it still supports our lives; but we do not know it. We have repressed it, it has become unconscious; and—though objectively speaking it remains positive and creative—from the viewpoint of our Ego it appears as negative, destructive, threatening the Ego. Together with the repressed collective powers it seems to constitute a fiendish group of evil spirits, endangering the Ego with passions and addictions, errors and blunders, too much or too little emotion, and worst of all, with a rising flood of half-conscious anxiety.

Anxiety may be defined as the opposite of creativity. It is the power of creation flowing in the opposite direction: creation being a centrifugal force; anxiety, centripetal. In the state of anxiety the intensity of life increases but its scope decreases. Consciousness becomes keener but its contents disappear. Anxiety is the opposite of life in the normal sense of the word; and, at the same time, it is the opposite of death, if death means quietude due to complete absence of consciousness.

Our creative center, the Self, is our positive relationship to God. Our Selfhood is the experience of our dependence on and our support by the Creator whom we know only partially. We realize creative power if we live from our real center. Then we are channels of creation. If we lose our Selfhood and our positive relation to the Creator, we are cut off from any new influx of power. And the power which is left, as it were, flows back into eternity. This ebb of creative power is what we feel as anxiety.

III

IMAGERY

1. The History of Images

History reveals the development from collective or tribal consciousness to individual consciousness, and at the same time, of course, from tribal to individual responsibility. Yet looking more closely we see that this is not a simple change or transformation. Individualism does not replace collectivism (as our individualistic philosophers have assumed). It is a process of differentiation rather than of substitution. Collectivism remains the basis of all human life, and individualism is added as something new. As long as the new attainment, the independent "I," lives in conflict with the tribal forces it must repress them into the unconscious. Yet by doing so it disowns its very source of power, the real center of life, the Self—and the result must be a split between Ego-consciousness and unconscious collective powers. This is what has happened to our occidental civilization.

The task now is to reintegrate the conscious mind with the collective powers without losing the achievements of individualism. The collective powers have to be admitted into consciousness so that the gravitation point once more may be the real Self, the "We-Self" instead of the individual Ego. The psychological difficulty of our task is evident. We are controlled—in our actions almost entirely and in our thoughts largely—by our Ego-pattern. How can we discover the real Self, how can we test our own ideas concerning the Self, as long as our egocentric eyeglasses show us only a distorted picture of the world and our thoughts are prejudiced by all the cunning tricks of Ego-preservation?

The solution is given in the fact that the good is always a unity while the evils are many. There is one real Self and there are many Egos, one truth about the world (even if we are able to see it only "as in a mirror") but many contradictory Ego-philosophies. They fill the history of our civilization. And looking at ourselves we see that our own Ego changes. Our Ego-pattern of today contradicts our Ego-pattern of ten years ago. This enables us to write the history of human character, which is largely the history of evil and deviation, and to understand our own history as a painful toiling from the greater to the lesser mistake. Yet even this slow and costly progress, and our understanding that it is progress, is possible only in so far as and because the real center of our lives, our relationship to God, is never completely cut off.

The history of our collective images as revealed in mythology, folklore and art shows a continual tendency towards petrification. Powerful conjurations degenerate into meaningless formulae, artistic styles into mannerisms, religion into superstition, and faith into mere intellectual creeds. Where this happens we always find a parallel development in the trend of collectivism towards individualism, and in the substitution of the Ego for the tribal Self. We have to understand the history of character—indeed the backbone of the history of mankind—as a dynamic interplay between consciousness and creative powers, with the history of our inner images as their result.

What the eyes see is conditioned by the eyes as well as by the object they observe. If the eyes degenerate, the things also appear degenerated. The degenerated Self, the Ego, when looking at the collective powers, will perceive degenerated images. From the kind of images which are seen we may draw conclusions concerning the egocentricity of the consciousness which saw them. To the same degree that the Ego grows rigid, narrow and shallow the powerful images are replaced by lifeless conventional pictures, empty allegories and mere intellectual concepts.

The tribal consciousness, the Group-Self, in the beginning of history is familiar with the collective powers. The gods and demons are beyond doubt and they can be propitiated or exorcised. The half-egocentric consciousness—as we find it in the Middle Ages—knows virtues and vices, but it has forgotten how to handle them. The new-born Ego can neither control the powers nor protect itself from them. They seem to be partly outer forces, like angels and devils, and partly our own human qualities, like passions and fears. The problem of responsibility is insoluble. At that time the images become allegories—love is a beautiful woman, loyalty is an anchor—giving a very poor description of the powers which they represent. Their remoteness from reality is shown by the fact that these allegories provide no means of dealing with the hidden powers. There is a gulf now between the powers and their symbols, just as there is a gulf between the Self and the Ego.

The most important instance is the image of the Madonna. It has been developed out of old, pagan virgin goddesses by early Christianity. And for a number of centuries it was powerful enough to enforce a definite change in the structure of the human mind. History, as we see, influences our imagery, and our imagery in turn influences history.

During the Rennaissance the Ego grew up to its full strength, and the allegories were replaced by clearly defined concepts. The concepts were shaped in perfect conformity with outer reality; this was the beginning of natural science. But on the other hand, these concepts were not able to describe the real structure of the human mind. Psychology is not a natural science.

Therefore all our "scientific" theories about human life do not enable us to influence this human life. On the contrary the scientist who has studied the whole literature, for example about love-life and sexuality, is the most awkward and helpless of all lovers. He cannot control his own powers (he usually represses them) nor can he lead the powers of others, either in his own love-life or in the cases where he is asked for advice. The distance between theory and practice has become almost insurmountable.

The average scientist of our times investigates reality from the viewpoint of the average egocentric consciousness. All his experiments are made with egocentric people.

His viewpoint does not allow him to discover the non-egocentric powers. And therefore he is convinced that the egocentric facts which he sees are the only facts which exist.

Wherever the impact of the non-egocentric powers interrupts the flimsy system of the scientist's theories, he immediately offers an egocentric interpretation which belittles or eliminates them. He calls the great passion a freak of nature. The fathomless anxiety of the insane is just a pathological symptom. Clairvoyants are impostors. And world wars are the achievements of some criminals who should be interned. Shallow as these interpretations are, they satisfy the egocentric consciousness and enable it once more to withdraw from reality. No wonder, therefore, that the ivory tower of philosophy, psychology, and theology now wields infinitely less power than did the Exorcisor ten thousand years ago, or the Delphic Oracle in ancient Greece.

It has often been said that the development of the moral sciences lags far behind the progress of the natural sciences. This statement is true, but it does not yet reveal the reason for the deplorable fact. The explanation seems to be that the egocentric consciousness is necessarily extravert. The Ego is interested first of all in its own defense. Therefore it watches the outer world to anticipate dangers, and to find weapons. And it cannot allow itself to turn inwards. It would discover that it has no independent reality and that it is only part of a larger unity. But the belief in its independence and self-sufficiency is the basic factor of its existence. Therefore, all the means of thinking and all the philosophical categories since the Renaissance are appropriate for the mastery of the outer world, but provide no adequate tools for grasping or controlling our inner realities.

Thus we come to the conclusion that the ancient tribal consciousness at once understood and misunderstood the collective powers of gods and demons such as Mars and Venus, Hecate and Medusa. The egocentric consciousness of the last century perceived the same collective powers psychologically as instincts, drives, and neurotic symptoms. Yet the borders between the different kinds, expressions and areas of power, though they always remained somewhat cloudy and overlapping, did not change considerably. Mars is now described as aggressiveness or "fighting spirit"; Venus became libido; Hecate is now called anxiety and Medusa symbolizes a bad conscience.

We are not better off, however, with our proud psychological terms, than our ancestors were with their gods and ghosts. On the contrary, they had practical ways of dealing with their gods. By worshiping Venus they could influence, increase, decrease or alter the power which Venus represented. By reading, thinking and talking about libido we can do nothing. We are much more in the grip of unconscious powers than they were, because our psychological terms are less "real" than were the mythological symbols. Therefore our danger, helplessness and suffering are stronger than ever before in history. A new start is necessary and—thanks to the creative stirring of the real Self—possible.

Our Ego-shell is breaking down, our egocentric eyeglasses are shattered. History is developing in a way which differs from the way that we had expected. The collective powers are moving in a direction which we had thought impossible. Yet the result of this painful disillusionment is magnificent. Our consciousness is able now to shake off our Ego-pattern sufficiently to grasp the new vision of life, nearer to reality than the scientific terms, more powerful than the ancient gods—a vision still incomplete, it is true, still seen "dimly as in a mirror," yet efficient enough to inaugurate the new historical era: the synthesis of collectivism and individualism, the unity of brotherhood and individual responsibility.

2. The Inner We-Group

We know not only generally that the individual needs fellowship and withers if he does not find a place in a congenial group; we know specifically that his group relations are preconditioned by special instincts, desires, fears, expectations and hopes, many years before they are actually brought about. His readiness to function as a member of a special group is developed and limited by earlier experiences in similar groups, and finally based on inherited functions and innate capacities.

In animal life the collective power which we call, for want of a better word, the "mother-instinct" controls the relation of mother and child. In human life this collective power is highly differentiated. The mother has developed consciously or unconsciously a special image of what her child should be like, and this ideal or idol controls her day dreams and her wishful thinking many years before the child arrives and it controls her actual behavior when the child is there.

From the original mother-instinct has been derived not only the image of the child but also an image of the desirable mother, although this may be more unconscious than the former. We find practically always two corresponding images which, as a unity, control the relationship between two members of a group. Husband and wife, brother and sister, children and parents, teacher and pupil, are the simplest examples. Our emotional reactions, our decisions and judgments, are much more conditioned by our imagery than by philosophical principles or theoretical convictions.

These images represent power because they are based on fundamental instincts. The whole life of a woman may be at stake if her mother-image is not lived out. But the special form of the image can be shaped by outer influences, education and self-education. In unfavorable cases it can be changed into its opposite. The woman may be afraid of having children. And the man, her possible partner and father of the child, may appear to her as a vicious criminal. In that case we may say that her behavior is controlled by a distorted feminine image, a sort of spinster- or nun-ideal, and she projects the image of a brutal Don Juan on almost every man. She is caught in the image-degeneration of her egocentricity.

Mutual understanding and creative group life have to be based on undistorted inner images which represent the true collective powers of the group. The best way to describe this peculiar and important relationship is to refer to the most natural kind of We-group, the family, in which there is father, mother, son, and daughter. Each member is endowed with special capacities and develops them (consciously or unconsciously) according to his position in the group. The two masculine members are more aggressive and daring. The two feminine members are concerned with the necessities for the welfare and harmony of the home. The two adults feel the responsibility for the future, and make preparations for the days to come. The two children do not think of tomorrow, but help in the engrossing tasks of the moment, enjoying life as it is.*

Each member, though different from the other members, instinctively knows their needs and desires. This knowledge is due to the presence within each person of the whole set of collective possibilities. The father has consciously developed his active and determined masculine attitudes. He knows what it means to be an adult man, because he is one. The image of masculinity has materialized in his life. At the same time he knows, half consciously, what boyhood is. He remembers his own past, and tries to give his son a better boyhood than he had. The image of boyhood is alive within his mind.

He knows also what womanhood means. The more his masculinity is developed the more he realizes what femininity means. His inner image of the woman first appears as his longing for a counterpart of his own self. Then it is the discovery of the real feminine nature. (Adam "knew" his wife Eve.) But this discovery is possible only on the basis of his expectation and anticipation; the image must

* Compare Diagram I, page 264.

first be there. Therefore the healthy man who is not blind towards his inner imagery instinctively feels what his partner likes and dislikes. He knows how to please her, woo her and conquer her, not by yielding to her, but by being her powerful counterpart—and in a similar way his instinctive image of the girl enables him to be the right father for his daughter.

There are always pairs of images related to each other. Adam presupposes Eve; and the more a woman represents Eve, or is conditioned in her life by the Eve-image, the more she instinctively knows about Adam, and his needs, desires and foibles. Her Adam-image will be powerful, too. If one of the two images is weak, the other cannot be strong.

The inner equilibrium of the healthy human mind, in childhood as well as in adulthood, may be described as the co-existence of many pairs of opposite attitudes and pos-sibilities. In the child's mind the temporary excitement of a play or a fight may be in the foreground, but in the background there remains the peaceful home and all the security of life represented by the image of the unchang-ing and reliable parents. Their images mean protection; they guarantee the inner equilibrium, and at the same time they represent unlimited growth and creativity. The images of brother and sister contribute to the same effect. The dim consciousness that the family exists and will help in all emergencies, or the unconscious conviction that the family remains a unit in spite of casual quarrels, consti-tutes the We-experience as the basis of brotherhood and mutual responsibility.

In a similar way the adults are not only conscious of the existence of their children, they not only remember that children and relatives are there. They know and respect half-consciously the needs and wishes, the values and possibilities, of all the members of the group. Here again the inner images are present and efficacious as inner conditions in the individual mind. We cannot get rid of them. They constitute duties and obligations, but also possible helps, hopes, and anticipations. A large part of our conscience, our natural feeling of loyalty, and the whole zest of our life is based on the existence of this imagery.

The We-experience is conditioned by our inner images which represent the members of the group and are at the same time parts of our own minds. Therefore we understand that the We-experience includes not only loyalty to the group, understanding of group life and confidence in group protection, but also an inner equilibrium, meaning the coincidence of calmness and courage, of serenity and responsibility, of caution and faith in awareness of danger.

The We-experience and its inner equilibrium prevents all superiority and inferiority feelings. In a We-group the adults do not feel superior; they understand and acknowledge the incomparable creativeness of the child. The child does not feel inferior; he realizes his own importance as well as the importance of all the other members of the group. The inner balance of the individual minds coincides with the equality of right and value among the members of the group. Here again the psychological structure of the group and of the individual mind reflect and condition each other.*

Now we know what it means that the members of the group are "represented" in the mind of the individual. Consciously or unconsciously everybody carries within himself the images of brothers and sisters, of friends and enemies, of husband and wife, of leaders and followers. To project an inner image on an outer individual means to love or to hate that person, with all our conscious or unconscious strength. The father has his family within himself as well as outside himself. He represents them because their images are organs of his mental organism; and they fill his life because the things that happen to them in the outer world happen to his inner world also.

3. EXAMPLES

The men who make history are those who—consciously or unconsciously—turn the switch on the inner switchboards of human character. They arouse, change, develop or repress the collective images of large groups and replace indifference by enthusiasm and fear by courage, or love by hatred and creation by destruction. Before we study the differences between positive and negative images, however, we should consider some examples which may show us the dynamic of the historical process.

We have to begin with simple cases from everyday life. Yet there is no doubt that they reveal the same principles and the same patterns as the great events on a nation-wide scale. Whether we study the psychology of teaching,

* Compare Diagram I and its explanation, p. 264.

preaching and political propaganda, or the influence of literature and movies, newspapers and paintings, we find always the same three problems: how to break down the egocentric shell, how to release the collective powers, and how to lead them into new creative channels. Or, putting it more briefly: how to replace the old outworn Ego-controlled imagery by new, more powerful and more creative images.

For our first example, let us go back to one of our earlier illustrations. In the case of the teacher and the rebellious class (Part II, pp. 63–4) we can assume that the teacher's Ego-image was formed in accordance with the ideal of the successful educator mastering the problems of discipline and wielding complete authority. This ideal was based only partly on the teacher's actual functions, capacities, and desires. For the rest, it was derived from theories and books and from the expectations of the Supervisor. Therefore it did not work. Not knowing her own unconscious power, she acted like a driver unfamiliar with her car. In speaking of courage and patriotism she stepped on an accelerator she had never noticed before. It was collective power that she touched off, both within her own unconscious mind and in the minds of her students as well.

There was an enthusiasm in her voice and a flame in her eyes when she described the heroic fighter. The image of the hero arose, charged with the courage of her unconscious instincts. It conjured up the corresponding images within the students. And for a short time she was Joan of Arc and they were her knights. But then she became afraid of her own excitement. Her Ego interfered and she became the teacher again—an angry teacher defending her own authority. The knights, betrayed and deserted by their leader, turned into rebellious marauders and felt hatred and contempt for the teacher who frustrated their best impulses.

Within each individual, teacher and students, we see the rising flood of the collective power. But it remains without leadership; no conscious Self identifies itself with this force and therefore it misses the creative channels. In the place where her maturing Self could grow we find her rigid Ego, afraid of losing its security. And instantly, on the side of the students, the Egos avail themselves of the powerful but not yet organized heroic images, distorting them into rascals and mischief-makers. The teacher wants discipline; the students want freedom; both fight for egocentric superiority and on both sides the gallant forces of courage and sacrifice are misled and misused in the service of the egocentric goals. They change into the negative: anger here, and chaotic riot there. The result is destruction.—The Ego without knowing it is always fighting on the side of evil and darkness, although it pretends to be a servant of light.

If the teacher had been mature and courageous enough —an almost superhuman assumption in the light of the general state of our civilization today—she could have had an experience of creativity rather close to a miracle. She would have enjoyed her own enthusiasm as well as the growing excitement of the class. Like a sailor in the storm, she would have forced the wind and the waves to serve her creative purposes. Her real Self would have taught her what the right purpose was. A new idea would have sprung from her imagination. A new vision, a new image would have arisen. And the problem of discipline would have disappeared since a new creative action would have absorbed all the emotions and thoughts of the class.

She might have found herself unconsciously beating time, catching the rhythm of the excited students, and might have burst into song. Some enthusiastic, gay, yet daring ballad, the true expression of the hope, the courage, and the fearlessness of all, including faithfulness and readiness to sacrifice, might have been the result. The Egos would have vanished and—for a short time—the real Selves of the individuals would have merged in the Self of the Group. But this short time would never have been forgotten again, either by the teacher or by the students.

Let us imagine a similar example: a speaker and his audience. It does not matter whether it is a teacher and his class, or a preacher and his community, or a politician and his listeners. All of these situations show three outstanding psychological possibilities. Other possibilities exist, of course, beside the three, and mixtures and transitions between them may occur too, but the three are the most important ones theoretically and practically.

(1) The speaker theoretically propagates the decrease of the Ego. But without knowing it he is as egocentric as his hearers or even more so. He is the unfit leader towards a more powerful life, and he achieves the opposite.

(2) The speaker favors the increase of egocentricity and he is at least as egocentric as his hearers. He is the fit and successful leader towards a pseudo-life.

(3) The speaker is less egocentric than his hearers and

he intends the decrease of their egocentricity. He is the fit leader towards creative life.

In the first case, the speaker wants to arouse in his audience all the enthusiasm for all the good and high ideals that mankind has ever known. He has studied all the ideals; he knows all the details; he is master of all the techniques. But one thing he does not know, and that is his own egocentricity. He is convinced that he does everything for the cause to which he has consciously committed himself. If he would understand that unconsciously he is striving for private success and prestige, that he cannot stand defeat, and that therefore he must misuse the great words and the high ideals in the service of his hidden egocentric goals—he would break down. It would mean moral defeat; and he cannot bear defeat. Therefore nobody can convince him of his egocentricity except those powers we are talking about. And even they need years and years to lead him into his crisis. For the time being, he still has a good conscience.

He tries to serve the good cause, but actually he serves his own Ego, and this he can do only by serving the Egos of his hearers. He must avoid their criticism. Therefore he tells them what they want to hear. And if they want to be blamed he blames them, but he does not lead them into their crises. All serious danger for their egocentricities has to be skirted. He only repeats what they already know: that they are bad sinners and that they have been saved; or that they should be good citizens, should not mind paying taxes and sacrificing their lives for liberty, for their country, or for mankind.

This speaker certainly uses big words in a beautiful way. And all the words point to an image which is supposed to be powerful, helpful, and the remedy for all our troubles, whether he calls the image the good citizen, the healthy man, the good Christian, or even Jesus. It is the only image which is available in his inner structure, the only inner value that his Ego can see, and therefore it is the everlasting subject of all his speeches. Yet it is an empty, powerless, and boring ideal that nobody cares for.

Something should happen during the speech. But nothing happens. The words are ignition-devices; they should start movement in our imaginations. The images should come to life; and the collective power—destructive first, and creative later—should burst through the egocentric crusts of frightened hearers like a volcanic eruption. But nothing happens. The ignition does not ignite; the images do not come to life and the collective power does not explode. Instead some people watch the time, some yawn, and some begin to whisper about their next bridge parties. Oh yes, they recognize that it is a wonderful speech, but they whisper nevertheless. And when the speaker finally begins to thunder, he has that deeply moving tremolo in his voice which conveys the message from his unconscious to theirs: "I am talking about the death of the Ego. But don't mind, my Ego is as clever as yours; we shall not do any harm to each other." The Egos are satisfied—and bored. Like a fleet of yachts in a dead calm, the Egos are lingering with slack sails. Nothing happens, except that the words and images used in vain lose a little more of their original contact with the collective powers.

Here the Egos are almost completely separated from the Selves, just as the images are separated from the powers. The images and all the words which refer to them are empty rhetoric; they are like paper money in an inflation. The more of them you produce, the less value they have. The speech therefore does not stir up any repressed power; and that means it cannot bring about the crisis of the Ego and lead the hearer closer to his real Self.

The next case shows the opposite situation. The speaker is at least as egocentric as his hearers, and he either enjoys it consciously or, if unconscious of it, would not mind finding it out. He propagates the alliance of all the Egos in a special group or even all over the world. The real powers have to be avoided. And the best way to do this is to ridicule them. Love is as ridiculous, therefore, as courage and self-sacrifice. Venus is a funny glamour-girl or a harlot or a boring and pseudo-scientific conception. And Mars is an obsolete superstition, the hired mercenary of capitalism, or an insane and infantile boy who should be committed to an asylum. And religion? Religion is idolatry and idolatry is ridiculous anyhow. All this is sugar for Egos but it is not yet enough to make a success.

The Egos nowadays do not feel quite at ease in spite of their apparent carelessness. They have a dim notion that life may be against them. Therefore they want to know what to do. If you could show them in a trustworthy way that "the Ego always finds a way out" or that "Old Adam survives all danger" the Associated Egos would pay you any price. The recommended subjects for your talks would be: The Way to Success; How to Become Rich; How to

Find Sexual Satisfaction; How to Exploit your Friends; How to Escape your Enemies. The psychological essence of the long list is simply: How to feed your Ego without paying the price for the food; or even more bluntly: How to cheat God. One topic is missing in the long list, namely: How to Die Egocentrically; or How Can the Ego Face Death? If some one could solve this problem he would be a stupendous success. Death, however, seems to be the only thing which we cannot cheat. And the successful book about Euthanasia of the Ego will never be written.

In this second situation the speaker and his hearers take their egocentricity as the undisputed highest value of life. They try to move farther and farther away from the real power and the real Self. Their spiritual force is therefore limited to the poor remnants of original power which they find in traditional images and superficial words. But the speaker uses this second-hand power so skillfully, and he spreads it out so thin, that everybody enjoys his wittiness and laughs at his shrewd and ready play with words. But his success does not last because it does not help in actuality. He has no real power and very soon, after having made a fortune, he will be forgotten.

There is, however, another more powerful and more dangerous variety of egocentric rhetoric: the idolatrous one. The full understanding of this kind of propaganda will be possible only after the psychology of idolatry has been studied in detail. Here it may suffice to say that the idolater consciously renounces his Ego, replacing it not by the real Self but by a sham-center, the Idol. The egocentric hearer, when forced to give up his Ego, usually prefers to replace it by the Idol rather than by the real Self, because he instinctively feels that the Idol may open a back door and allow the Ego to slip in again.

The third situation presupposes a speaker who is less egocentric than his hearers and who wants to lead them nearer to the real Self. He has to arouse their collective powers and this can be done only by forcing their Egos into a crisis. They will object, of course, and defend their egocentricity as much as they can. But he has a strong ally in their collective powers which he knows how to find. He may use the same words as the man in the first example but he puts them together in a different way. Now they point to a different image which is alive within himself and not too deeply asleep in his hearers. But they do not yet know this image; they have never seen it clearly, or if they have seen it they misunderstand it for the sake of their Egos.

His words awaken this image within their unconscious minds. It is the image of a strong and almost reckless creative power. It includes self-sacrifice, creativity and humbleness. It contradicts their egocentricity. They feel uneasy and want to repress it. They call the speech "silly, embarrassing, heretical, revolutionary." They wish to leave but their excitement keeps them there; they already feel that they have to defend their Egos on two fronts.

On the outer front, there is this speaker who oversteps all bounds of traditional acquiescence, or—if he happens to be a politician—of the traditional shouting and praising or blaming the government. He neither shouts nor praises nor blames. But he tells the truth with unbearable exactitude. He tells what could be done and why it is not done. He describes the futile tricks of the Egos, telling his hearers what they feel at the moment and why they feel it. Their egocentricity becomes visible to themselves. They are aware of their deficiencies; and embarrassment vies with the incipient smile of a new freedom.

The new and powerful image against which the hearers started to fight constitutes the inner battlefront. It becomes the inner enemy, now independent of the outer enemy, the speaker, who brought it to life. They may run away from him and never hear him again. But they cannot escape the inner enemy, the image, which is his partner and which is part of themselves. The discovery of this inner battlefront creates the crisis. The Ego ceases to be the almighty sovereign of the inner life. The opposition grows and the revolution begins.

But this new image appears as the inner enemy only as long as the individuals identify themselves with their Egos. The next moment, they may remember that they always felt a longing for a better and deeper life. They wanted to be more selfless and more completely committed to their cause. But they wanted to achieve this by self-control and moral practices. Now another avenue is open towards this goal. It comes from inside themselves, not with moral commands but with creative power. It is really their better Self. And this better Self is more than their individual lives; it is We, it is love; and more than all this, it is He.

The most amazing thing is that this new and unheard-of power is at the same time well-known and familiar to them. They have felt, thought, dreamt all this many times. Only they were never able to express it clearly enough. Now the speaker's words have appealed to this thing which was ready to awake and to rise from the unconscious into consciousness. But still it is incompatible with the former structure of their lives. When the new power arises the old form of life, their egocentric character, explodes. Then there is a moment of breathless anxiety. They are afraid that the chaos will destroy them. And then the most unexpected thing happens: a new clarity and certainty, and a new and deeper consciousness are there; the real Self and its creative forces begin the new work.

It is not yet the Kingdom of Heaven. It is only the first step, a very small step in this direction. But it proves that there is a way; and even the smallest step forward on this way gives us new power and new creativity.

IV

DISINTEGRATION

1. THE EGO AND ITS SHADOW

We have described the original We-group which is usually, though not always, identical with the family. And we have mentioned the early "breach of the We," the destruction of the child's We-experience, when the egocentric adults betray the We-feeling child. This catastrophe, we said, causes the child to replace his real Self by an Ego-image. From this point on his life pivots more or less around Ego-preservation and Ego-enhancement.

Thus, every We-group dissolves sooner or later and more or less thoroughly into egocentric individuals, and afterwards is maintained only as long as the egocentric interests of the members are better served by staying together than by scattering. There is no inner power, no living loyalty which could protect such a "sham We-group" against eventual decay. And it is important to realize that in this connection morality is powerless. The group is recognized only as long as the Egos can profit from it. To the degree that its members are egocentric no sacrifice for the sake of the group can be expected. On occasion, outwardly good behavior can be enforced by sanctions which would endanger the Ego's own interest—hence the system of reward and punishment in all egocentric societies.

We have said that the members of the We-group—before the breach of the We—are represented by inner images within the conscious or unconscious mind of each member. The "inner We," the set of images within the individual, corresponds to the "outer We," the group of individuals. It is for this reason that the center of the individual, his highest value—or better, his source of values—coincides with the real center, the highest value and source of values, of the group. The inner images within the individual are balanced around the same hub as are the actual individuals in the outer world. This hub is the real Self; although the members of the group may call it variously "our cause," "our mission," "our way of life," and sometimes even "our God." It is the source of power and creativity which enables both the individuals and the group not only to meet all outer challenges but also to solve creatively all conflicts between the inner images and their contradictory interests. The mother may be torn between the baby that needs its diapers changed and the husband who needs lunch. Only her creative center, observing and combining the two inner images, husband and child, can solve this problem and turn impending irritability into laughter and creative comedy.*

Now, the question arises as to what happens to the inner imagery of an individual when the outer We-group breaks down. His real center is replaced by an Ego-image. The gravitation point is shifted, the hub is superseded by an

* Compare Diagram I, p. 264.

eccentric and artificial "highest value," namely Ego-preservation. The real Self—which is not an image and can
never be seen or influenced as if it were an image—seems
to disappear or to be entirely blacked out. The images,
however, cannot vanish. They will remain, if not in the
conscious mind then in the unconscious.

We have already seen that images can be repressed, that
they can deteriorate, lose their power, or turn into the
negative. But we do not yet see what this fact means with
regard to the relation between the individual who harbors
the decaying imagery, and his fellow-men in the outer
world. In order to answer this question we have to begin,
of course, with the special image which becomes the new—
and wrong—center of the egocentric individual, the so-
called Ego-image.

The Ego-images are rather simple, at first, expressing
immediately the Ego's pretended superiority or its fear of
being inferior. "I am the good son of good parents"—the
Ego-image of feudal or moralistic aristocrats—simply
means "I am better than others, and this is (or should be)
proved by my blameless behavior." "I will reform the bad
world, including my bad parents" means: "I am better than
everybody; not the superiority of my tradition but the new
self-evident value of my own personality is the basis of all
my claims." Feudalism has been replaced by rugged individualism.

Before the breach of the We, the child does not know
the difference between good and bad. He only knows that
he is "the little boy," an essential part of the group and in
harmony with all its members. Then the requirements for

membership in the group are raised, and raised again. He is supposed to eat spinach; not to eat the applesauce first, though it was on the table all the time; to clear away the toys; not to wet the bed;—and all this seems to be the arbitrary command of a dictatorial adult rather than a genuine need of the We-group. At the very beginning, in the cradle, it was quite different; the paradise is lost. —Shouldn't he rebel? Why comply with the whimsical adults? To hell with the group if the group means losing the paradise!

The innocent "little boy" image has split, has differentiated, into two little boys of opposite value. One is the "good boy," siding with the adults, in harmony with the group as it is or ought to be now, and ready to sacrifice, forget or repress everything which interferes with the inner peace of the group. The other is the "bad boy," a rebel, a daredevil, and if necessary a criminal. To him life is worthwhile only if it is lived recklessly and dangerously, defying the adults, scoffing at their dreary morality, acknowledging no standards, no authority, enjoying all kinds of mischief and sabotage, laughing even at pain and death—the negative hero, loyal only to his Ego-pride and, to some extent, to his fellow-gangsters.

The moral differentiation of the original images is as old as mankind. The motif of the two fighting brothers, one good and one bad, is to be found in primitive religions, myths, and fairytales all over the earth. In the Old Testament it recurs almost like a musical "theme with variations." There are Cain and Abel, Abraham and Lot, Jacob and Esau, Joseph and his brothers; and on the feminine side, though less elaborate, Eve and Lilith, Sarah and Hagar. In depth-psychology we call this motif the problem of our negative (inner) twin or the Ego's shadow. And we assume that since every one has an Ego-image every one probably will have its counterpart, the negative Ego-twin-brother or Ego-twin-sister, too.

In a few cases the twin images remain equally conscious and available. Some children are extremely good when at home and extremely bad when with their playmates, or vice versa. They live as it were in two different worlds alternately. But usually one of the images is consciously and officially accepted while the opposite is rejected, condemned, and repressed into the unconscious.

The good boy develops all the qualities which seem to be desirable for harmony with the adults; he is as they want him to be—or rather, as he thinks they want him to be. This attitude becomes his second nature. But the other half, the bad half, of his first nature still exists. There is a slight possibility that he may "forget himself," that is, forget the ideal image of the good boy, and have a tantrum, or steal some chocolate, or take the radio apart, or put a frog in grandma's bed. The bad twin, the Shadow, turns up like a ghost, haunting the good child and asserting that—fortunately—the other half of reality is not entirely lost.

From the viewpoint of the Ego the resurrection of the bad twin means utmost defeat. The whole Ego-pattern would explode if we would acknowledge that this bad behavior is as natural to us as the ideal Ego itself. Therefore, to preserve the Ego, we call it "not I," my weakness, my vice, or the devil. The proper psychological name is the Ego's Shadow.*

The Shadow is a possibility of behavior and experience which completely contradicts or excludes the consciously acknowledged Ego pattern. If your Ego ideal is to excel in smartness, fine clothing and brilliant conversation, then your Shadow may be illustrated by the following scene: You come to join a party on a rainy day. Your car has to stop three feet from the curbstone. You try to jump, elegantly, in front of seven well-dressed ladies who look at you in admiration. You jump, you slip, and there you lie in the mud in your new evening clothes. For the one who wants to be rich the Shadow is his extravagance which makes him poor; for the ambitious one it may be ridicule; for the spoiled child it is exposure. It is the "dog-house," the situation which makes us wish to be swallowed up in the earth; and usually it is the unavoidable result of our egocentricity.

From the viewpoint of depth-psychology, as we shall see, the acceptance of the Shadow means honesty and confession, and leads to the experience of forgiveness, which is the only way out. But under the tyranny of the Ego there

* The term "Shadow" is taken from the Jungian Psychology. (Cf. Frances Wickes, *The Inner World of Man*.) We use the word in a more specialized sense than the Jungians. To us it means the crystallization point of all the powers which are repressed into the unconscious. The term "Ego" is used by Jung in approximately the same sense as we use it. The only difference is that we ascribe to the Ego certain unconscious functions which serve its purposes while Jung uses it exclusively with reference to consciousness. The "Self" for us is a metaphysical reality which exists not only all through the individual life but also beyond space and time. Jung thinks of the Self as an entity which comes into existence only through the process of integration. We would say it awakes, or should awake; he would say it should be brought into existence through our personal development.

is neither honesty nor confession nor forgiveness. There is
only condemnation and fear. For the reconciliation of the
twins would transform both of them, and the reign of the
Ego would come to an end.

The Ego-image seems to represent all the desirable
values of life—honor, righteousness, power, reputation, or
security, wealth, and indulgence in all the good things.
The Shadow, on the other hand, appears as a symbol of all
that is repulsive, detestable, and unbearable. In both cases
the image symbolizes our own attitude as well as the
outer situation. If the "dog-house" is represented by disgrace, it does not matter whether the individual is disgraced
through some fault of his own or through outer circumstances; but it would not be felt as disgrace, it would not be
"Shadowy," if the Ego-image were not endangered by it.

On the thermometer of our egocentric values, the ideal
Ego-image marks the point $+$ 100; the negative twin, the
Shadow, corresponds to the point $-$ 100. If we know one
of these two points we can determine the other one with
almost mathematical exactitude.

In this way our egocentric striving for $+$ 100 (superiority or security) and fear of $-$ 100 (inferiority and insecurity) are related to our inner images. And since even distorted and deviated images are still channels of power we
may understand that our egocentricity, together with its
Shadow, is strong enough to wreck not only individuals but
groups.

2. Unfolding Unity

The increasing interplay between the human being
and his environment—people, animals and things—en-

forces the unceasing development of the individual's inner world. This inner world, in its thoughts and feelings, tendencies and desires, fantasies and fears, and—as we may now add—in its imagery, in part mirrors the outer world (for example, with regard to physical facts) and in part displays its own inner structure (for example, with regard to ethical and artistic values). Its growth can best be described in terms of unfolding (differentiation) and unification (integration).

There is, for instance, the unfolding of the child's knowledge. Insight is growing through progressive distinctions. Out of the fog of primordial We-feeling may first emerge the distinction between the child's own body and the rest of the world; or it may be the distinction between "We," namely, those who behave well (like the mother bringing the milk), and the rest of reality, behaving in a casual and sometimes disagreeable manner. Then there may follow the distinction between mother, *kind*, and mother, *sorrowful*, etc. Experiences leading to innumerable distinctions will finally provide a certain knowledge of complex facts which recur time and again (such as feeding, bathing, caressing) and which may arouse identical emotions on every occasion.

The same experiences, however, will cause the child to develop his attitudes, his abilities, his physical and mental functions, in order to influence the outer world. A turn of the eyes changes the aspect of reality. Pulling the blanket over one's head makes the whole universe disappear. Later it has to be learned that there is a difference between not seeing the toy while it remains on the blanket, and throwing it over the edge of the crib. Later again the difference will be discovered between walking and running, yelling and singing, and so on, ad infinitum. This is what we may call the unfolding of our capacities.

The most important development, however, is the unfolding of the inner imagery. We have mentioned already mother, *kind*, and mother, *sorrowful*. Then there may enter the distinction between brother and father, and later brother admiring the baby, and brother teasing him. Indeed, there are so many possibilities, distinctions, shades and unexpected changes that nobody could ever learn them and find his way through the labyrinth unless he had a sound and clear way of registering all the material.

The We-Psychology assumes, at least as a working hypothesis, that the child's system of storing and relating the material is rather simple. We presuppose certain points of crystallization connected with and based on innate instincts. These latter have the tendency to develop into images representing the biological relationship between the members of the natural family. They enable the child to react adequately, for instance, to friendliness or anger, long before any conscious understanding can be expected. The child very early recognizes similar attitudes. All dignified men are "papa," all friendly animals are "cat," all hostile animals "bow-wow," dogs. The images are the first "pigeon-holes." Their growing development enables the child to distinguish, to remember and to "label" with increasing subtlety his inner and outer experiences. Therefore the wrong distinction of early images will result later in wrong scientific systems and wrong philosophical categories. The right distinction of images is the indispensable foundation of subjective truthfulness and objective truth.

The best example of the development of an important image, as observed in practical life, and that means under the influence of egocentricity, is of course the development of the Ego-image. "Little child" is split up into "good child" and "bad child"; or sometimes, without the moral implication, into "wild child" (the later conqueror extravert) in the morning, and "dreamer" (the introvert, the later poet or philosopher) in the evening. The bad boy may be unfolded into "bad boy successful" (+ 100) and "bad boy caught by the father" (— 100), and so on.

It seems to be a fundamental law that every inner image is or should be balanced by its counterpart, just as our muscular system is balanced. The movement of the contracting muscles has to be smoothed by the cooperation of the stretching muscles; one nerve accelerates the heart-beat and at the same time another nerve calms it down; and so forth. The same seems to be true wherever we find life. Balanced couples of opposites are needed to guarantee the process of self-preservation as well as procreation and further development.

However, balanced pairs of opposites cannot be kept in function by separating the extremes. The image of the good and the bad boy exclude each other, and to keep them in mind, in balance, and to make them cooperate requires another psychological function, and in many cases a conscious additional effort. This function we call "integration" or unification.

To understand the exact meaning of the term "integration" it is advisable to think first of the opposite process: "disintegration." The wild boy in the morning tends to forget that he is a bookworm in the evening. The good boy with his parents may be quite different from the same boy when he is with his gang of classmates. In these cases the opposite images ("wild" and "quiet"; "good" and "bad") are more and more separated; and finally one of them will be repressed into the unconscious while the opposite controls the conscious behavior. This is disintegration.

In some cases disintegration can reach the point where two different personalities are developed within one person, without knowing each other and almost without interfering with each other. This, of course, is a pathological condition. But many average and normal people, without being neurotic at all, show a similar oscillation between contradictory attitudes without being aware of their inconsistency. A girl of seventeen may be a very calm and reasonable person when with her parents or in the schoolroom. The image of the "good girl" prevails. But as soon as her lover appears she is changed, fascinated, hypnotized, as if under a spell. Her inner glands and her sympathetic nervous system seem to function in a new and maddening way. Don Juan has conjured up the image of the gypsy, the "bad wild girl"; and she defies parents, school, church and police until the spell is broken and the "good girl" comes to the foreground again.

It is interesting to see that such a girl can be conscious of her two different attitudes, but unable to control them, to unify them, or to choose between them. Disintegration here has not yet broken the continuity of memory and consciousness. In most cases, however, the incompatibility of our different images compels us to banish one of them into the unconscious and to accept the other one as our sole and exclusive pattern of life. The inconsistency of the images, then, is stressed and increased by their division into the officially enthroned image which now definitely becomes the Ego-image, and its rejected counterpart, now becoming the Shadow, down in the limbo of unconsciousness.

This disintegration of the inner imagery is the usual destiny of the average individual in our time. And we know that further disintegration on both sides will follow. The conscious Ego-image, usually overdeveloped, deteriorates into rigid allegories and empty but high-sounding abstractions, while the unconscious Shadow remains underdeveloped and therefore turns into the negative, creating fear and anxiety.—Disintegration results from egocentricity, and destroys human life just as the decay of living tissue ensues wherever a malignant tumor develops.

The opposite process, the re-acceptance and assimilation of repressed images, should be called "reintegration," or "reunification." It will be described, at least to a certain extent, in Part Three of this book. For the moment it is sufficient to discuss the function of unification as the counterbalance of unfolding, and the ideal result of their interplay: "unfolding unity." The unit exists first: the whole is prior to the parts, as, for instance, a fertilized cell, which then splits into two, four, eight, sixteen cells, building an embryo. The outer layer of cells, later the skin, is already different from the inner layer, later the intestines.

That is unfolding by differentiation. But the oneness of the whole prevails, expressing itself in complete cooperation with the different cells and organs. Later the whole is unified even by special organs such as the nervous system and the blood vessels, representing, as it were, government and communication. As long as unfolding is balanced by unification we have an ideal organism: unfolding unity.

In the realm of our psychological life, and especially after the development of conscious and unconscious images, this balance of unification and unfolding becomes increasingly difficult. Original unity and further unification are not, of course, entirely missing in the development of the average individual; but we have to admit that our civilization, possibly for the last thousand years and certainly since the Renaissance, has been characterized by too much unfolding or differentiation, and insufficient unification or integration. The result, as we see, is the increasing disintegration of individuals and groups.

In the ideal case, the case of "unfolding unity," two opposite images such as the "good boy" and the "bad boy" are distinguished but not separated. Their functions are developed as different possibilities, related to different outer situations; but they remain the activities of the same individual, and the boy feels free to choose between them. He is not carried away by his Ego-image; on the contrary, he remains himself, and the image serves as a kind of rôle or costume which he wears as long as he wants it, and changes when another costume seems more desirable. This is the psychological basis of all creative plays of smaller children and of many (but not all) daydreams of adolescents; they develop their capacities by playing rôles, identifying themselves with different images at different times.

The less the moral implication in the image of the "good" and the "bad" child has been underlined by the adults the easier it is to develop the "virtues" which are contained in both of them and to drop the "vices" which they include. The good boy may help mother when she cleans the house; he learns to handle dishes and to repair mechanical defects. The bad boy is accustomed to yell, to stamp his feet and to fight for his toys when little sister wants to steal them. Yet if the neighbor's big dog attacks little sister in the back yard, the bad boy immediately wages war against the intruder. His customary yelling turns into the battle-cry of the crusader. The stamping of his feet is replaced by skillful and daring kicks. He hits the dog and chases it out of the yard.—Be sure of this, that if you had not allowed the bad boy to stamp his feet you could expect no gallantry or chivalry when the enemy attacked little sister.

If you repress the image of the "bad boy" you cannot develop the image of the courageous defender of justice in later years. The fighter for justice, even if he is merely a mental or spiritual fighter, needs the courage which is invested in the image of the bad boy. The good boy is not courageous; he has learned only to conform to the majority. The image of the "fighter for justice" has to combine the daring attitude of the bad boy with the good boy's concern for the group; and it has to drop the bad boy's disregard for the interest of the group and the good boy's fear of disapproval. The result would be creative re-integration.

Poor parents! If you favor the good boy and repress the bad one you bring up an egocentric coward, a mere conformist. If you want to raise a gallant fighter for justice and liberty you must allow the bad boy to yell and kick. How will you check his mischief, prevent his egocentric deviation, and make him use his courage in the service of creative goals?—We can do this only by developing our own creativity. Indeed, our children will show exactly the same percentage of integration and disintegration as we possess ourselves. Only the children usually reveal their difficulties more openly. Older people are more successful in hiding them. By our fruits we may know ourselves.

3. Love and its Caricature

The ideal family is united by two facts. First, the four members, father, mother, son and daughter, have the same inner imagery. For them, the father-image, for instance, is "collective" not only in the general sense that they feel about fatherhood in vaguely the same way that all the races and all the centuries have felt, but that they have a quite definite idea concerning the rights and duties, the capacities and limitations of the father. Their father-image contains a complete inventory of the father's character and of all his relationships inside and outside the family. Since this image is identical within all of them there is no misunderstanding, no quarrel or doubt. The collective images of the members of the group are not open to any controversy—or development. (Here we begin to see that the "ideal family" is ideal only in a timeless ideology, and that it is not ideal at all in reality, that is, in time, and in history.)

The second fact is that the father himself is controlled by the same father-image (his leading image) which the others use unconsciously when they speak to him, or think of him, or take care of his needs. Therefore nobody will be disappointed. The father really behaves as they expect him to behave, he lives their father-image; and they behave as he wants them to do, because their attitude towards him is conditioned by their leading images (son, daughter, mother) which represent the well-balanced counterparts of his father-image.

Thus the imagery, in the ideal case, enables us not only to understand each other, and to act as the group wants us to act: it establishes our need for each other, our mutual participation in sorrow and joy, our compassion and collective responsibility. We are not happy, none of us is happy, as long as one of us suffers. The sound imagery in a group of sound people is the essential organ of psychic communication between the members. It presupposes, of course, that not only the images are identical, but also that the real centers of the different individuals coincide, that they are a real We-group. Otherwise the images could not remain in harmony with each other.

At the same time the imagery is a channel, or better a system of channels, through which the creative power of the real center mobilizes all the capacities of the group. Imagine that in a primitive We-group the daughter has been insulted by enemies. Immediately the whole group is aflame. Rage and courage, resourcefulness and determination are almost limitless. And the girl, without outer information, knows exactly what her relatives will do. She cooperates with them because she is moved by the same imagery. The whole group acts "as one man."

Here we see what our imagery as means of wordless communication may achieve. It conveys not only insight, understanding, information, but also power, courage, love, hatred, patience, fortitude, endurance, confidence and unending hope. All this, however, is true only in the ideal case—which scarcely exists nowadays. What we actually see is different. On the one hand we find the egocentric deterioration of conscious images and their mummification into allegories and meaningless words; and on the other hand, the repression of the more powerful images into the unconscious, and the negative development of the pent-up powers into vices, diseases, and other means of destruction.

There are instances, however, which allow us in spite of our egocentricity to experience the original function of our images as means of human contact and channels of creative power. They are to be found in the realm of reintegration. The best-known example is the so-called "great" love between man and woman. A man and a woman, let us say, are egocentric to a not unusual degree. Their mutual images of Adam and Eve are distorted and stereotyped according to the average pattern of public opinion. He is looking for a glamor girl; she wants a successful and smart lover with a new Buick and a good salary. She identifies herself with the glamor girl, and he has no difficulty in playing the rôle which she wants him to play. Both, however, are just playing rôles; they live a secondary and indirect life; their real centers are still asleep. They are not creative at all. Yet they seem to be a good match, being equally egocentric and superficial.

Imagine that they have a serious accident. Each one has to risk his own life to save the other. There may or may not be a moment of conscious hesitation. Then he knows he will rescue her or die with her. And she does not even think of the risk she has to take for his sake. Both images—the glamor girl and the smart lover—have disappeared in less than a minute. Her face will show scars all her life; he will be disabled for many years. It does not matter. Death has touched them. And the threat of death is the best, and in some cases, the only, friend which can destroy our Egos and awaken our sleeping centers. And in so doing it immediately restores the original imagery.

The young man looks at the bleeding face of his wife. And suddenly he sees what he never saw before: she is not a glamor girl, she is a woman, thoroughly human and thoroughly feminine; and in that moment she is helpless and miserable, but brave, very calm, and, astonishingly enough, happier than she has ever been. She watches him, and discovers for the first time in her life what a man really is. His proud mask is gone; no assumption, no pretense is left. He is really himself, and infinitely better, more modest and more powerful than his most successful rôle. Now at last they know each other, and they know that they are one.

Their mutual images now are in open contact with

each other and with their real centers. He looks at her, he feels "Eve," and is vaguely aware of all the experiences and all the hopes which man has ever felt in the presence of a woman, all through the history of mankind. But through her womanhood, which he discovers like a limitless treasure, he sees more: he sees her real Self. And she, being recognized in her center, and understood in her human dignity, in spite of her human deficiency, now feels her own dignity and her own center, which she so far has never been able to find. And she is able to see his real center, to understand him, and to make him understand himself. Now they experience the mysterious power of the word "We." The We can now be described as the central contact of two individuals which is established through two corresponding images and results in a complete and almost irresistible circuit of creative power.

When the real Self is replaced by the Ego the original function of the images as means of genuine contact and expression of creative power is superseded by a new function which can easily be understood as Ego-protection. The boy in our earlier example (page 85), after the painful breach of the original We, neither comprehends nor loves his father; he is afraid of him, and tries desperately to find a way to avoid his anger. What the boy knows about his father, for example, that he is more accessible after dinner, and that he smiles when you pretend to be honest, is used only as a weapon of diplomacy; and the earlier experiences of course are applied to later situations of a similar kind. But this application of earlier experiences is subject to a peculiar and dangerous limitation; it is as rigid and mechanical as all our egocentric functions are.

Let us assume that the boy one day expressed emotions, perhaps joy or hope, which infuriated the father. The breach of the We became evident once more, and the child erected within the egocentric pattern the inexorable law: "I must not show any emotion, or else . . ." This law becomes part of the code which now controls his relationship to his father, and this code is part of the Ego-image, "the secluded boy." The image and its code remain in force for years or decades; they become what we call the child's "second nature"; and will persist long after the originating circumstances have changed entirely.

These rules of behavior are too rigid, too much generalized, and too blindly applied in a compulsory way and without discrimination. Because the father behaved once or twice in this manner he is supposed to behave so all the time. The experience of one outstanding incident is *transferred* as a pattern of reaction to all cases which seem to present a similar danger. In other words, the image of the father, now the deteriorated, egocentrically misinterpreted image, becomes unchangeable. And all the boy's "laws" of behavior, expressing his fear, distrust and helpless dependence, may be derived logically from this rigid image which has become a terrible caricature of a father.

The earlier experience sets the pattern for later experiences, not only with the father himself but also with other people in a similar position. The boy *transfers* his expectations, prejudices, fears—in fact, the whole father-caricature—to teachers, bosses, superiors, and all representatives of authority. And by doing so he almost forces them to behave as if they were what he expects them to be. His distrust irritates them. Finally they explode, and he thinks: "I knew; they were not trustworthy." And his distrust grows.

Transference is the indiscriminate, mechanical, and usually unconscious application of childlike behavior-patterns towards different people in similar situations. It contains especially expectations, hopes and fears which are often connected with strong emotional reactions. It cannot be improved by reasoning or changed by new experiences, because it is based on genuine and powerful images, even though these images have been changed into egocentric caricatures.

Transference operates from the viewpoint of the Ego and in the service of the Ego. It is reasonable and comprehensible from the standpoint of Ego-valuation, yet it becomes ridiculous and gives the impression of blindness or callousness as soon as we look at it objectively. Suppose you have been spoiled and protected by an indulgent mother. You transfer her image (the mother caricature) to your wife. She, however, expects you to protect and spoil her. The two transferences clash. Terrific emotional reactions ensue. Both partners feel betrayed, both suffer; neither is able to discover his own mistake.

Where we transfer the egocentric caricature of a genuine image to one of our fellow-men, we replace our central contact by an egocentric though unconscious presumption which violates our partner's real Self, and in many cases even his Ego. He must disappoint us—and indeed he should. Only the collapse of our whole ego-centric pattern can help us to replace the transference of rigid and weak caricatures by the powerful and creative contact of genuine images.

NEGATIVE LIFE

1. THE WRONG EGO-IMAGE

The most destructive feature of egocentricity is its rebellion against time. Complying with time means growing older and more mature, slowly and patiently. It requires creativeness, or at least flexibility. The egocentric patterns, however, are rigid and defend with fearful stubbornness the momentary Ego-image without admitting any possible change. Sometimes the Ego-image is related to the future, but it is not therefore less rigid. "I will have this kind of family, this much money, this much influence." What the future has to be is decreed arbitrarily from the viewpoint of a timeless but egocentric valuation. The Ego, as we said, tries to be God; God is beyond time; therefore the Ego does not submit to time. To wait, to fail, to grow old, to die, is unbearable for the Ego. And the worst of all words for it is "too late."

Suppose the Ego-image in a certain case is "good little girl." By the time the child is four or five, this limited and one-sided image constitutes already a grave error. It would be better for her if, in addition to being the sweet and admired little pet, she would act occasionally as a nasty little mischief-maker. Ten years later she is still the nice little girl; her Ego-image, being rigid, has not changed; she speaks and feels and acts like a precocious child of about five. Older people think she is "cute," and the aunts praise her for being virtuous; but the boys don't like her. Again ten years later, her Ego-image is still five years old. She cannot grow up. She is good and kind and meek, but she cannot stand any difficulty, nor can she take responsibility of her own. And thirty years later she is a completely ridiculous creature, a white-haired baby, trying desperately to be cheerful and "cute." Her Ego-image is entirely out of tune with reality.

Cases like this are rare, fortunately; but they occur. However, in a more diluted form, we find this sort of "arrested development" in every egocentric personality, which means practically everywhere. The Ego-image is located in a position in the inner We-group where it does not belong. The mother may have the Ego-image of a little girl. The father may behave like a youngster. And, looking more closely, we find that more intricate Ego-patterns outnumber the simple ones. A mother, for instance, may live emotionally on the level of a child; mentally she may be mature but completely masculine; while physically she is a healthy woman of her real age.

The opposite sin against time is possible too. A small boy may anticipate the dignity of fatherhood (especially if his father lives the life of an egocentric child). The boy then does not learn that he is the "little one." On the contrary, he finds out, by practical experiment, that he can have his way, if only he screams and yells loudly enough. The child, of course, does not know what happens; the psychologist, however, may see unmistakable signs of the "choice of the wrong Ego-image." There is a look in the boy's eyes and a tone in his voice which at the age of two already herald the future boss or dictator. His whole attitude says, "You do what I want you to do, or I smash you!" His father, the sissie, admires the aggressive boy. His unlived life, his repressed desire for power, his inner twin brother, seems to become reality—in so mild a form, and without any danger to the father's effeminate Ego. So the father lets him have his way.

Later the father understands that his boy will do in earnest what he, the father, never could do because his egocentric pattern did not allow it. The daredevil, the egocentric conqueror, develops with amazing rapidity. Now the father is afraid, he despises the boy's behavior. He terms it bad taste, or even immorality. But preaching does not help; and punishment increases the evil. The boy is and remains the bully. He takes the place in which the father should have stood. He is the shadow of his father's Ego, materialized in the outer world.

Psychologically speaking, if in the outer We-group the place of the father is empty, then the father-image in the child's imagery is, as it were, "unemployed"; it does not find a lodging place in outer reality; so it becomes easy for the boy to identify himself with the vacant father-image, and to transfer the image of the sissie boy to his father. Thus he anticipates the advantages of adulthood without paying the price, that is, without accepting the disadvantages such as responsibility, hard work and sacrifice. The egocentric pattern, then, shows a second mistake in addition to eccentricity and rigidity, namely the wrong location of the Ego-image.*

Unfortunately this mistake of anticipating the future cannot be corrected by time. Thirty years later the boy will be just as immature a bully as he used to be at the beginning of his egocentric career. The father-image which he assumed as the "ideal" of his Ego was not that of a grown-up father. It was an egocentric father caricature. It was distorted from the very beginning; and it will be more distorted thirty years later. He may have children, then, but he will bully them and exploit them, and force them into another kind of egocentricity.

Yet the choice of the Ego-image can be even worse: it can confuse the masculine and feminine side of the family group. The girl may feel that it would be much better to be a boy. As a boy she would be allowed to climb trees and to go with her brother's gang to steal apples. If she is very discouraged she decides that she is and has to be a girl, which means that she feels inferior, insecure, resentful and bitter. (All girls are "bad," then, in the sense of inferior, underprivileged.) But if she still retains some courage she decides: "I will be a boy. Believe it or not: I *am* a boy!"

She identifies herself with the image of boyhood as she finds it within her imagination. She talks her brother's slang, walks like a trooper, throws things around as her father sometimes does, and refuses flatly to knit or to play

* The pattern of the "wrong location" of the Ego-image is shown in Diagram II, p. 267. The practical case there, however, is opposite to the case described above.

with dolls. Of course, this masculine Ego-image may be remote from real boyhood. The negative features, such as roughness, swearing, and even cruelty, are exaggerated, and the positive ones, chivalry, helpfulness, endurance and fortitude, are missing. The image, however, is usually strong enough to change the girl into a complete tomboy. And even the inner glands are sometimes influenced to a certain extent so as to retard puberty or to decrease the development of breasts and hips.

In the opposite case the boy would understand that life is too dangerous for him, and that girls are less exposed to this danger. So he prefers—especially if the place of the "big boy" is taken already by an older brother—the Ego-image of the girl. He becomes a sissie, and in the extreme case, a homosexual. He avoids fighting and calls his cowardice a Christian virtue. He cannot stand disharmony, and terms this weakness a love for peace. He develops good taste, a definite sense of beauty, but no patience and no efficiency. Physically, of course, he remains a man, but his potency is usually underdeveloped, though he may consider himself as highly sexed.

In some cases the picture is more complicated. The Ego-image is then masculine in one layer and feminine in another. The boy may be a sissie physically and emotionally, but a bully or even a tyrant mentally; or vice versa. And the girl may be very masculine in her mind as well as in her physique, while emotionally she may be over-feminine (the type of certain hysterias); or vice versa. The respective Ego-images may be the oversensitive scholar, the prize-fighter, the emotional suffragette, and the sentimental mother. The right image has to be discovered in every case individually. All generalizations are wrong.

There is no limitation to the choice and the combination of our Ego-images. Every place in the family scheme of father, mother, son and daughter can be usurped by every member of the family. But life becomes the more miserable for ourselves and for our fellow-men the further our Ego-image is removed from our natural position in our group. Moreover, the strangest mixtures of images occur, real monsters with the sweet intentions of an angel and the cruel appetites of a devil; and, as we said before, different images can be used at different times.

We can easily imagine, now, the extreme case of a completely reversed family. This caricature may never occur in reality; but again we have to say that less severe cases of this kind, with more diluted egocentric intoxication, are not so rare. The father plays the rôle of a helpless little girl; he is oversensitive and needs a guardian to fight off the hardships of reality which he simply cannot stand. So he has married a tomboy whose Ego-image happens to be a tramp. He mistook her carefree behavior for strength, and her big words for reliability. Later she turned out to be totally unreliable, which made him feel even more insecure and therefore inclined to lean on his eldest boy. This boy learned very early that he could not trust his parents. They could not help him. Therefore he does not trust anybody but himself. At the age of five he is already a tyrant; at ten he assumes the leadership in his family and at fifteen he is the undisputed and completely egocentric boss. His younger brother, being excluded from government and power, excels in stunts and jokes. He amuses the whole family and makes them laugh when the inner conflict becomes critical. Like a mother he preserves peace, but he does it on a merely egocentric basis. Because everybody likes him or even needs him, he is allowed to do as he pleases. He takes the best sweetmeats, gets the finest clothes, and is as touchy as the prima donna in an old Italian opera.

The four members of the family are equally egocentric. And the Ego-image of each is in an opposite place from its rightful one. The father is an egocentric girl. The mother is an egocentric boy. One son is the egocentric father, and the other is the egocentric mother. They will torture each other until all their egocentricity breaks down.

2. TENSION AND INHIBITION

When people complain about their inner difficulties such as nervousness and irritability, or inhibitions and fears, they frequently use the word "tension," or similar expressions derived from the same root. They say, "I am tense, I cannot relax, my nerves are highly strung." And their outer appearance reveals that they are right. They frown, they clench their fists, their movements are abrupt, and they easily develop intestinal cramps. Even where physical symptoms are missing the intensity of their speech and the defensiveness of their reactions seem to indicate some kind of mental or emotional tenseness as the underlying evil of all these more or less "nervou " attitudes.

Here "tension" is evidently something bad, something to be avoided.

In other cases the same words are used with an opposite meaning: people complain of not having enough intensity. They are slack, listless, indifferent; and they wish to be more interested, more intensive, more tense. Or they say that the intensity of modern life wears out their nerves. They cannot bear so much tension, they are not strong enough. And if the stress and strain persist, a nervous breakdown may be the result. Or a married couple confess that they do not feel any sexual tension, and that this lack of tension is lack of love, or at least lack of happiness. Here "tension" means something good.

All these expressions are borrowed from the "tension" of the strings of musical instruments. If the strings are too tense or too slack the instrument is out of tune. Our nerves have evidently been misunderstood as resembling musical chords. But with reference to the more complicated picture of the human mind which we have developed in the foregoing chapters we need a more careful terminology. Therefore we will use the word *tension* with regard to the Ego and all its manifestations. (For example, the ambitious student is tense and his tension endangers his success; he should learn how to relax.) And *intensity* will be used in relation to the real Self and the inner images as far as they are still (or again) in genuine relation to the center. (A man and woman who are intensely in love with each other feel not only the growing intensity of their own relationship, but of all their functions and reactions in life.)

The complaint that modern life is too intense for our nervous constitution has now to be formulated in a rather disconcerting way: Life is intense; it demands the creative reactions that issue from our real Self. If an egocentric person tries to meet this demand he may succeed for a certain time with the help of reckless cunning and tricky devices, but sooner or later he will fail; his Ego will be endangered; he will feel tense, irritable, nervous, and finally he will break down. The less he is egocentric or the more he overcomes his Ego and brings to light his real Self, the more he will be creative, intense and equal to the task. His presence of mind will increase the intensity of life—and make it less comfortable for his egocentric fellow-men.

All egocentric tension can easily be traced to our striving for superiority and fear of inferiority. We survey a task, and the more we are afraid of failure, the more we overestimate the energy which is needed. Here is a piece of black wood, weighing one pound; you mistake it for iron, expecting it to weigh some ten pounds. In lifting it you not only spend unnecessary energy jerking it up too fast and too high; but you also waste energy reestablishing an artificial equilibrium between the upward movement and the downward pull. In our example you would have to add a downward pull equal to nine pounds by straining your own antagonistic muscles; otherwise the movement would be uncoordinated and probably a failure.

Imagine a person walking easily and carelessly along a mountain path. Suddenly he sees a sign saying that there is danger of a landslide. He discovers the cracks and crevices across his trail; he begins to move with utmost care, slowly and cautiously. He spends ten times as much energy for each movement as is necessary; therefore his muscles are tense, his breathing is irregular, and where he should walk fast and lightly as a dancer would do, almost without touching the ground, there he is going step by step resting his whole weight on the unreliable soil. And worst of all, the more he is aware of his mistake the less he is able to do better. He is caught in the vicious circle of egocentric fear, and only a miracle can save him.

Most people are psychologically in exactly the same situation when they try to pass an examination with outstanding grades, or to apply for a job which they desire very much. If they were less anxious they would meet with more success. And many people—not only neurotics but normal average people—live on a general level of egocentric tension high above their natural intensity. To them every new task and every normal day mean an additional strain. A vacation means only relief from this *additional* tension, not the disappearance of their habitual amount of tension. They always behave as if they had to carry a load of fifty pounds on their shoulders. The normal work of everyday life to them means ten more pounds; they carry them faithfully, and after having done the job they are glad to be freed from the additional ten pounds. But the invisible fifty pounds remain; they try to rest, but no genuine enjoyment, no thorough relaxation is possible; and finally they are glad when the vacation is over and they can shoulder the additional ten pounds again.

What are the mysterious fifty pounds of habitual tension? They represent our egocentric fears, based on our unconscious central anxiety. Since our creative center, our real Self, is out of commission we have good reason to feel insecure and inferior. Every moment life may ask us: be creative! answer this question! invent something new! solve an unheard-of problem! And we would be completely unequal to the task; not because human nature is not creative enough and the task is superhuman and therefore unreasonable, but because of our own egocentricity.

Here is the point where our feeling of inferiority coincides with a vague but very deep and genuine feeling of guilt. We are not "legally" responsible for our egocentricity. Yet we have to bear its consequences. Life confronts us with the checks which our ancestors have signed and we have to pay. "Be creative; overcome thy Ego and theirs; or perish!" We may consider this unjust, unfair, impossible; we may rebel with all the little strength which our Ego still possesses. Rebellion only creates new tension and therefore makes things worse. If we could recognize the higher (namely, collective) responsibility and the super-individual justice which controls human history, we could easily cooperate with the creative powers of life and our sickening egocentric tension would be superseded by living intensity.

Theoretically it would be possible to annihilate the Ego and dissipate its whole system of defense mechanisms within one minute of horrible crisis. It would be a sort of spiritual death, the breakdown of the whole past, all valuations, fears, and hopes, and the immediate birth of a new life. We do not know whether this has ever happened. The classic example which is usually quoted in this connection, Saint Paul's conversion at Damascus, seems to prove the opposite theory. His egocentric pseudo-religion certainly was critically challenged by the death of Stephen; and his "breathing out threatenings and slaughter against the disciples" is a significant symptom that his inner crisis had already started. He "made havoc of the Church" because the Church was making havoc of his Ego. That is the pattern the Ego usually follows.

The long period of incubation preceding the crisis is due to the fact that our Ego develops in the course of time the elaborate system of defenses which we have already mentioned. The citadel of the Ego is surrounded by strongly fortified barricades and pillboxes, just as the real Self is surrounded by powerful images which may be understood as secondary power-stations. The difference, however, is evident: the egocentric fortifications serve a merely negative purpose, the defense of the Ego. The original images, on the other hand, are the positive expression of creativity. We cannot even say they serve the Self; because the Self, if it is real, serves the group and through the group, God.

The creative power of the real center, as far as it expresses itself through the channels of our undistorted imagery, is realized subjectively as the intensity of life. Its significant qualities are colorfulness and aliveness; and even if things are going wrong there is a sense of the presence of immediate value. The same power is subjectively felt as tension if it is misused in the service of the Ego. It

may help to postpone the fate of the Ego, and may therefore evoke the sensation of triumph or pride; but it always
destroys life and therefore carries a vague feeling of bad
conscience. Tension is always concomitant with uneasiness
and imminent danger.

The outer line of egocentric fortifications consists of
rigid rules and regulations which can easily be understood as parts or functions of the Ego-image. We usually
call them *inhibitions*. The good boy, for instance, learns:
"I must not fail; I have to avoid all disapproval of adults;
I must win the highest praise, outwit my rivals and secure
the first place in every contest." These laws unfold new
implications almost every day. *Differentiation** is working
as fast on the negative side as it does on the positive.

The boy learns that he cannot take any risk unless he
has the complete guarantee of success. And if certain situations prove to be treacherous with regard to this guarantee they are simply written on the black list of things
that must not be faced. To recite a poem, for instance, may
be dangerous in spite of the most careful preparation.
Some criticism might still occur. Then the Ego had better
decide not to talk any more before any audience. The
decree is issued, the machinery of Ego defense is geared
accordingly, and—the result is a speech-inhibition which
prevents this dangerous situation with the precision and
thoroughness of a perfect automaton.

In a similar way the same person may be prevented
from saying "no." To reject an invitation, for instance,
would mean to provoke disapproval. This has to be avoided
at any cost. So the invitation is accepted, though it may

* *Cf.* definition, p. 120.

include the necessity of speaking to an audience. The Ego, now, can neither refuse, nor do what it is asked to do; it is caught in the intricacies of its own legislation, thus proving that further development on the negative side only leads deeper into the tragedy of Ego-destruction.

The original positive imagery is consistent. Wherever its development leads into apparently insoluble problems, a new and creative idea may turn up and provide an unexpected and astonishing solution. One of the best examples is Jesus' answer to the Sadducees' question concerning immortality (Matt. 22:23–33). But the Ego-image is not creative. Its development is artificial and shallow. It is as if a small amount of color were spread out too thin. The color loses its tone, becomes weak and insignificant, and finally disappears completely.

The same is true with regard to all the other inhibitions. Some people cannot make decisions, some cannot show their feelings, and some cannot feel at all. Others cannot think clearly and others cannot stop thinking. Practically any function of body and mind can be at least partially inhibited.

Sometimes the inhibition hits a function which is constitutionally weak, and sometimes one which is exceptionally strong. A person, for instance, with a definite inhibition in the field of mathematics may have a mathematical endowment far above average, or far below. No test can prove which is the case; but careful analysis of the unconscious structure may reveal some vestiges of our "hidden talents." And only the collapse of our Ego, the central crisis, can bring them to life again.

3. BLUNDERS AND CRISES

Wherever two tendencies of the human mind contradict each other we find the danger of blunders and bad habits. Suppose a girl has a boy friend who usually sees her home when she leaves her office. She decides to give him up, and with much effort writes him a letter that he should not come any more. Her decision is reasonable, but her feeling runs counter to it. However, when she seals the letter she feels relieved; she has done the right thing. Next day the boy is there, waiting for her as usual. He has not received the letter. She is furious. Finally she finds it in her hand-bag. And immediately she knows: "I forgot to mail it because I wanted to see you again! I hated to write it. Thank God I made this mistake!"

Here is a man going downtown. His wife asks him on his way back to stop at the grocery and to bring two pounds of carrots. His first reaction is, "Am I a messenger boy? Why doesn't she go herself?" Then he understands that she is busy with the children, and tired—of course he will be glad to help her. But he forgets the carrots, remembers them when unlocking the door, hurries back to buy them, and brings them triumphantly to his wife. She looks, and is offended: "I see I cannot expect the smallest help from you. Oh, of course you do what you can for me; you bring the carrots—but you don't help me at all! They are half rotten!" And she cries bitterly. She has understood his unconscious resistance, and all his reasonable excuses do not comfort her.

Examples like these can be found everywhere in ordinary life. There are no bad imps or benign spirits involved, stealing things from our pocket or our memory and restoring them when we deserve it. There is no need even to resort to divine guidance to explain these happenings. Psychologically they are not amazing at all. They are simple expressions of the fact that our unconscious is a little more alert, more courageous, and has better memory, insight, and foresight than our conscious mind.

The situation, however, is not so simple that we could say: heed all your hunches, obey every inkling of your unconscious, and you will be guided perfectly. Neither is the unconscious entirely wise and good while the consciousness is egocentric and bad, nor vice versa. The former is the wrong assumption of those who ascribe to the Holy Spirit all the thoughts which turn up during a period of prayer or meditation. They are just as wrong as the others who ascribe all interfering ideas to the Ego, or some evil spirit. The problem has to be investigated more carefully; it is exactly as intricate as the structure of the human mind itself.*

First of all, we have to say that not all blunders are significant. Many of them are valuable symptoms, it is true. They can and should be understood as tokens of our deeper desires (the case of the unmailed letter) or expressions of our discouragement (the case of the rotten carrots). In these cases the blunders indicate a tendency which at the time is unknown or unacceptable to the individual.

* It is the merit of Sigmund Freud to have discovered the deeper meaning of blunders. His interpretation, quite un-Freudian (that is, not yet related to sexual drives), is excellent, though not deep enough. (Freud: *Psychopathology of Everyday Life*.)

But we have to admit that in innumerable cases the mistake may be merely casual, that is, caused by irrelevant circumstances such as fatigue, ill-health, or interference of other occupations.

If you forget to mail a letter, the reason may be an unconscious or half-conscious desire not to mail it, or incipient influenza, or the sight of a beautiful woman who catches all your attention just as you pass by the mail box. Thus you can choose your alibi; you will always find at least half a dozen different explanations which are equally acceptable. But if you are hunting for the truth rather than for excuses you had better assume that an unconscious tendency was involved. And if you cannot discover it this time wait until the next blunder occurs.

The decisive insight which we may attain from the proper analysis of our blunders is due to their connection with the different strata of our mind. In the case of the unmailed letter, the girl's mother would say: "Your conscious resolve to send the letter was good, objective and moral; the opposite tendency, to forget it, was egoistic and bad. Under the disguise of forgetfulness your egoism got the better of you." Her lover, however, would say: "Your egoism told you to obey your family, to be the good girl, faint-hearted though apparently unselfish. But your unconscious instinct, your love, your daring heart got the better of you, and so you didn't mail this cowardly document."

The girl herself could probably find an even more bewildering inner situation. She might discover some egocentricity and some objectivity in both tendencies, to mail the letter and not to mail it. Her Ego wants some sexual satisfaction in kissing the boy in addition to a virtuous crown bestowed by her mother and aunts for giving up the sinful love affair. And on the other hand she sees objectively and honestly that there is real value in avoiding sensuous stimulation as well as in the further development of her sincere relationship with the boy.

The way out is difficult to see as long as we talk about tendencies, drives and needs. It becomes quite obvious, however, as soon as we relate the tendencies, drives and needs to their underlying imagery. The Ego-image of the spoiled girl is very apparent. She wants everything, satisfaction of the senses and of her religious ambition, the heavenly crown for her head and the thrill for her inner glands: the Ego-image is undoubtedly the spoiled child, the pet, "Her Majesty, the baby." And here again we see that the Ego-image produces contradictory claims and is not creative enough to reconcile them. Therefore it resorts to a special form of negative life, the blunder—a poor and sterile attempt to satisfy the two contradictory tendencies at once: to write the letter without doing so, to serve both masters, to be the sweetheart and the nun. And all this in complete innocence, without any consciousness of the Ego's refined diplomacy!

As far as the Ego is concerned it has caught itself in the meshes of its own net. There is no way out. But, as soon as we look for the objective and creative images which may be found in the deeper layers behind the Ego-image, the whole picture changes immediately. We call this process searching for the virtue behind the vice. We try to unearth the creative power-image behind the sterile Ego-image. And if we succeed it may help us to discover even the real center, the Self, behind the Ego, and thus to reverse the whole development of egocentricity.

The latter result, however, can be expected only if the blunders (or whatever the negative results of the negative life may be) originate so much suffering that a real crisis, the breakdown of the Ego and the beginning of a new life, becomes unavoidable. The blunder in such a case would lead to catastrophe, and what at first sight seemed to be a superficial mistake would turn out to be the fatal action which changes the whole life.

Suppose, for instance, that the girl in our example were to argue with her friend about the unmailed letter, and in trying to get rid of him, in a moment of utmost despair, she were to hurry across the street just when the lights change and a car knocks her down. Psychological half-suicides like this are not rare. They always show the exact structure of the blunder as we have described it.

During the crisis that follows, the Ego-image would lose its rigidity. The girl would "turn and become like a child," the real, creative, undaunted child rather than the spoiled pet. And the image of the growing, loving, conscious and conscientious girl would emerge and lead her to the simple yet creative discovery: "I love the boy, and therefore I want to see him. But we should not satisfy our mutual and egocentric desire for sexual enjoyment. If we cannot find a way of being together without going too far and too fast in our caresses—then we better quit until we grow more mature."

All his egocentric objections she would sweep away smilingly: "I hate the selfish little boy you are! Because I love the mature man you will be. Don't come to see me before you are a grown-up man!"

If you object that this creative and courageous attitude could not be expected from a young girl, you may be right. But this only means that usually a young girl in such a situation does not really face her crisis. She does not suffer honestly and does not know her own "heart's sincere desire." Neither her mother nor her lover can help her, both being equally lost in their own egocentric mazes. And life, being patient and kind, does not yet put her to the crucial test of being run over by an automobile. Therefore the girl probably will blunder along, serving two masters, writing letters and not mailing them—until her negative life in the course of the years heaps so many failures and disappointments on her shoulders that finally her Ego breaks down and she stops blaming others and begins to discover her own responsibility.

The Ego, as we have seen, is in a desperate position. Like a bad government it braces itself against outer troubles, but it chooses the wrong way, runs into inner troubles, and therefore collapses when the outer troubles grow serious enough. The inner difficulties which we have described as "negative life" are the result of our inner conflicts between the Ego and the repressed images. They provoke outer difficulties—and often just the kind of difficulties that they are supposed to prevent.

Our distrust induces people to leave us alone; then we feel betrayed, and think that our distrust was justified. Or we attract people by our excessive friendliness, then our repressed vanity explodes in an outburst of anger, or, even worse, hurts them secretly by half-conscious calumnies and unjust criticism. Thus, we unconsciously destroy what we consciously build; the weapons of our Ego-defense become the means which finally annihilate the Ego.*

The most dangerous of these weapons is the transference of earlier experiences to similar current situations in the form of rigid expectations, fears or claims. Generalized prejudices must lead to disappointment, quarrels, offenses and anger. If you believe that all teachers are hypocrites because your first teacher really was one, or if you expect all doctors to treat you gratis because your family doctor did so when you were a child, you will certainly run into trouble. Yet, less obvious and more subtle transferences may have an even more disastrous effect. If you pursue the unconscious policy of hiding your intimate feelings, because your elder brother used to ridicule them, this inhibition will poison all your friendships and stifle your marriage.

Life asks us new questions every day. Our former answers have to be revised time and again. We must be creative, discovering new aspects of the truth, and developing new forms of life—or we will perish. A reaction which is right at the age of twenty may be wrong at forty; and a

* The so-called "suicide of the Ego" can be understood in many cases as the result of the Ego's one-sidedness and rigidity without resort to unconscious influences. In some cases, however, the interference of the Shadow is so evident that its contribution to the final development of the whole personality cannot be overlooked. The reason a drunkard drinks, for example, is only in its outer appearance egocentric: his Ego rebels against restraint. The real power of his vice belongs to the Shadow. Therefore he cannot be helped unless or until his Shadow is integrated.

principle of business or politics which was successful in
1925 may be disastrous in 1950. Time, the changing outer
circumstances, is against rigidity; egocentricity, the artificial inner equilibrium, is rigid, because rigidity seems to be
its only means of survival; therefore time will destroy the
Ego, the changing outer circumstances will abolish the
rigid patterns of our inner life.

The citadel of egocentricity is attacked from outside
and inside at the same time. The new outer situation which
requires a new adjustment, and the old inner conflict which
makes the new adjustment difficult, seem to cooperate
purposefully to defeat the Ego. Then the Ego musters its
last reserves for a last-ditch stand, and again the result is
a betrayal: the last reserves turn out to be enemies. The
student who has put off writing his paper until the last
day is caught in a vicious circle. The more afraid he is of
failure, the more tense he grows; his tension prevents creative work; he worries; time elapses, unused; his fear increases; and the final mobilization of all his will-power
creates only anger against himself, new tension, new excitement—and no work at all.

Many psychologists have observed the "law of reversed
effort" (Baudouin). It is usually described as the fact that
an unusual conscious effort brings about an opposite result.
The bicyclist who strives to avoid the stone will hit it. If
this were the whole truth the law of reversed effort would
mean the definite collapse of all ethics, moral education
and even civil legislation. The law tells you you should
not steal; you try to obey, and the very attempt to avoid
theft causes you to steal. This fortunately is not true, in

spite of St. Paul's experience, "the command gave an impulse to sin, and sin resulted for me in all manner of covetous desire" (Romans 7:8).

The "law of reversed effort" should be replaced by the "law of materialized fear." The bicyclist hits the stone not because of his desire to avoid it, but because of his fear that he may be unable to avoid it. His Ego-image tells him to avoid the stone; the Shadow whispers: You certainly will break your neck. If the Shadow prevails, the latter will happen. The fear of failure on the part of the Ego means distrust in its own strength and the growing conviction that its inner enemy, the Shadow, will one day win the upper hand. The Ego's fear increases the strength of the Shadow.

Here we are confronted with the central question as to where the power of the Ego and the Shadow originate, and which agency or rule is responsible for the distribution of power and therefore for the final victory or defeat. There is no doubt that the original source of power here again is the real center, the Self. The Ego, the Shadow, and all the other images, repressed or not, deviated or not, are mere channels of power. The more they preserve their original connection with the Self the stronger is their activity, whether conscious or unconscious. The more completely they are cut off from the Self the more they wither and finally become atrophic like the muscles in a paralyzed arm. The Ego-image is usually separated from the Self by rigid walls, and the conscious life of the egocentric individual therefore gradually loses its zest and creativity until finally he himself admits that he does not really live.

His life, as far as it is conscious and egocentric, becomes shallow, unreal and meaningless. The real center and the real value remain inaccessible to the Ego, behind the walls in the depth of the unconscious.

The Shadow is separated from the Ego by the same walls, which means it is repressed into the unconscious together with the real center. But the connection between the center and the Shadow is not seriously damaged. Therefore the Shadow does not wither. Its repression turns its power into the negative direction. It becomes destructive, as we have said, but it remains young, primitive and vigorous, like the oppressed peasantry in a feudalistic country.

At the beginning of the egocentric development, the different channels convey an equal amount of power. Ego and Shadow are balanced. Later the Ego declines in vigor because of its separation from the center, and the Shadow becomes comparatively stronger because, as we may now say, the center supports it, in spite of its negativity, while the Ego is gradually forsaken. This is why the egocentric person appears to be satisfied, successful and even happy during the first half of his life. Later, however, his rigidity increases, and his whole occupation becomes Ego-defense. The inner enemy, the Shadow, seems to grow, and the fact that it remains unknown (that is, unconscious) increases the danger. Then all kinds of doubt, skepticism, distrust, fear, hypochondria and anxiety foreshadow the impending breakdown.

The startling fact is that the real Self favors the Shadow in opposition to the Ego, in spite of the Shadow's destruc-

tiveness. Consider the drunkard. He may be a pious hypo-
crite as long as he is sober. Then he drinks. His Shadow
usurps the throne for a short time, yet long enough to
destroy thoroughly the sham-values of his egocentric life:
his reputation, his career, his family life, his friendships
break down. He cannot resist the temptation; in spite of
all this disaster, he drinks again. His destructive Shadow
is stronger than all his egocentric "good will"—because,
and as long as, his "good will" is nothing but an egocentric
device. He will lose the battle time and again; the powers
of evil, his addiction, will be stronger than his best purposes and his most holy promises—because, and as long
as, his egocentricity, hypocrisy, and self-deception are the
more dangerous evil.

The strategy of the power of life is far from being one
of acquiescence and appeasement. Life has to be lived,
and destructive life, bad as it is, is still preferable to seem-
ing death. Destruction arouses overwhelming forces on
the positive side, anxiety can be turned into creativity, and
hatred can be redeemed by love. But unlived life is worse.
To bury the talent is a greater sin than to misuse it.
Average egocentric people, "whitewashed tombs, looking
comely on the outside," are in their unconscious filled with
buried talents, repressed possibilities, which have turned
into the negative and now are "dead men's bones and all
manner of impurity." If we do not find an antiseptic way,
a religious way, to cleanse our tombs, the impurity will
come out into the open. That will be bad, but better than
the whitewashed lie.

Every egocentric person denies these statements, calling

them ridiculous superstition or unscientific speculation—unless he is sophisticated enough to accept them theoretically and to all practical purposes shelve them, together with other "interesting psychological remarks," by writing a book about them. If the statements are right, however, neither sophistication nor ridicule can invalidate them. Tension and sleeplessness, inhibition and irritability, will do their work. The hounds of heaven, by the Ego called the hounds of hell, will corner us. The crisis, the breakdown of the Ego, will begin.

Then all the disasters of human life seem to clamp down on us in the same moment. Our friends fail us; our health fades away; the doctor shrugs his shoulders, and his silence seems to say "cancer." Our opponents' lawyer starts a new lawsuit; our work lags and the boss is impatient. Well, we may know that most of this is our own apprehension, but the insight does not help us. We feel like a swimmer tossed about by the dark waves of the ocean, exhausted, hopeless, and about to sink.

In such a situation we are ready to pay any price. The slightest relief would be accepted gladly even if the whole Ego had to be sacrificed. Survival in any form, under any condition, even death itself, would be welcome, if only this nightmare, which has now become reality, would disappear—or if reality, now a nightmare, would only change.

And then, there are voices offering help. There are always several voices. And we choose one of them. It is no conscious and deliberate choice; we are worn out, tormented, and grasp the hand which seems to offer the quickest relief. And in almost every case the choice is wrong. We make a new blunder. We choose the tempters, the pseudo-saviors, the "false Christs, and false prophets" who "bring forward great signs and wonders" (Matt. 24:24, Moffatt). The crisis stops short of the utmost catastrophe, our anguish is relieved, our old individualistic Ego is replaced by a new ready-made group-Ego, and the second half of the crisis is postponed for a long time to come.

VI

IDOLATRY

1. The Idol

The psychological development during the first half of the crisis can be described as *regression*. The rigid prejudices of the Ego are melting away under the increasing pressure of perilous circumstances, and earlier, more childlike valuations are revitalized. A wealthy lady, for instance, may have been convinced for many years that she could never drive to a bridge party in an old, jolting Ford car. Unless she had a new Packard every year she preferred to stay at home. After her husband's bankruptcy she was actually sick and in bed for a year; two years later, however, she had learned to enjoy the shaky old Ford, and she felt better than in the days of the new Packards.

The Ego becomes more modest, more insecure, more primitive, though not more reasonable. The lady with the old Ford is now crazy about housekeeping. She dismisses her maid, wants to do everything herself, and spends hours figuring out whether it is more economical to send the sheets to the laundry or to buy a washing machine on the installment plan. The Ego-image of the sophisticated society lady has been replaced by the earlier image of the good housewife; but it still carries much egocentricity and is still threatened by a Shadow. For the society lady the unbearable situation had been: old clothes, imitation jewelry, and an unfashionable car. She had been forced to accept all this. And now her "abyss," the new Shadow, is exactly the opposite: to fail as a housewife, to spend a dime in vain, to increase the financial burden of the family. Her former social life now appears to her as an abomination.

The new Ego-image, which is historically a very old one, may be more useful for the time being. It may even represent a rather satisfactory adjustment to the new situation. Yet it remains rigid and based on fear rather than on genuine creative power. To bring about real reintegration, a further step in the direction of regression is needed. The lady has to become more definitely like a little child; and that means helpless, confident, and ready to do whatever life wants her to do. That is the second and more painful step on her way through the crisis; but it is still part of the first half of the journey.

Her friends warn her that she neglects her husband, as she neglects her make-up and clothes. He does not like housekeepers anyhow, so he may have an affair, one day, with a society girl. . . . And suddenly she remembers that several times he did not come home for dinner, on some futile pretext. . . . Here she sacrifices her youth and her beauty, doing all the hard work, and he betrays her! . . . Or does she exaggerate? Maybe she sees specters? . . . Sleeplessness, restlessness, distrust ensue. She feels forsaken, left alone in a hostile world. Nobody can understand her, nor does she understand herself. She is afraid she may go insane.

Her present Shadow, her former Ego-image, the spend-thrift, the society lady, turns up again, but now it is projected into the outer world; it becomes the rival, her husband's sweetheart. And she does not know whether this beautiful girl exists in outer reality or in her own fantasy only. In any case, it represents her own unlived life, her twin sister, who has to be accepted and loved. Now her crisis is at its climax. She is completely unequal to the tasks of everyday life, neither a housewife nor a society lady—nothing but a desperate child.

As if by chance, in one of her hopeless moods, she listens to a sermon or a lecture or a radio-address. Some one says: "All your fears and sorrows only indicate lack of love. If you could love you could forget yourself; you would live for the benefit of other people; and you would be happy." She knows this is true. She does not remember that she has heard and read similar ideas a hundred times —they come now as "the good news," the gospel, strikingly fresh and powerful. She feels an immediate relief, a vague dawn of new possibilities, new vistas of life, new security. And she writes a letter to the lecturer, giving herself completely to the new cause.

She is honestly ready to renounce her Ego, or better: her egocentricity is breaking down through its own failure, and she begins to feel dimly that she herself may be different from her Ego. The real Self is about to emerge. The rigid structure of her imagery and the system of values as

established in her early years, after the breach of the
original We, disappear. And reality, freed from the dic-
tatorship of egocentric evaluation, seems to whirl around
in a dizzying chaos of destruction and new creativity. She
does not know what is good and what is bad. Anything
is possible. She is a child, she needs a leader, a teacher, an
adult.

Then the answer to her letter arrives. She is accepted.
The "master" signs her membership card. She is one of
his many disciples. She is at home. He tells her what is
good and what is bad. He knows everything. He protects
her. Wherever he is, there chaos is replaced by peace and
harmony. She readily gives up her Ego. She understands
that all her egocentric valuations, desires and fears were
erroneous. But she had not known better because she did
not yet know HIM. Now he takes away all her doubts. She
is happy, healthy, efficient and ready for every sacrifice.
She is thoroughly reborn.

She meets others who have gone through the same experience: they are reborn, converted, saved, too. And she
enjoys enormously the new fellowship. There are drunk-
ards who stopped drinking three years ago, epileptics who
got over their fits, professors whose blood pressure went
down from 200 to normal, and truck-drivers who can
easily drive eighteen hours, now, though a year ago they
were fatigued after a half day's work. And she discovers
with amazement that she no longer asks whether her husband has an affair with another woman or whether she
spends a dollar too much for her laundry—if only all
three of them, her husband, his sweetheart, and the laun-

dryman, would join the movement and be reborn like herself!

The process of regression has reached the point where in early childhood the breach of the original We took place. All egocentric traits have gone. The Ego and the Shadow have lost their importance, and therefore both fear of inferiority and striving for superiority disappear. Even the demarcation-line between consciousness and unconsciousness is strangely slackened. The individual feels dreamy in bright daylight, and creative visions as well as forgotten memories loom in the twilight of consciousness.

But certainly not all those who turn and regress to the inner situation of early childhood will enter the Realm. In such a moment more than ever we are exposed to the "blind guides of blind people" who "traverse sea and land to make a single proselyte" and then "make him a son of Gehenna twice as bad" as they are themselves (Matt. 23:15, 16, Moffatt).

What happens in such a case may be described psychologically in the following manner: Regression clears away all the barriers between the images and the real Self. Creativity flows once more through all the channels of the collective imagery. And the whole process of development and education, of groping for a way and of learning from failure and success, would virtually begin anew—were it not for the "blind leader" who, like the parents in early childhood, seeks to impose his will and his judgment as infallible truth. He is there. We always find some one who gladly assumes this rôle; and we are more than glad to project on him the collective and powerful image of the Great Prophet.*

In most cases he is objectively somewhat nearer than we to the real center, which means that he wields more knowledge and power than we have been able to muster during our egocentric past. Thus, to a certain extent, he is fitted to be our teacher or guide. But we are not satisfied (nor is he himself) with his rôle as a temporary adviser. We find ourselves for the first time in our adult life in the immediate presence of our own creative center. We sense the burning fire of life and we do not yet know whether it will enlighten us or destroy us. And he interprets it, he explains our situation. He knows—at least we think he knows—the central fire, and how to deal with it. Through him we hope to find it when we need it, and he protects us if it threatens to burn us. He steps in between our real center and our bewildered consciousness (which has not yet found a new point of crystallization since the breakdown of the Ego-image). Instead of discovering that the real center is our own real Self, and that its nature and name are not "I" but "We" and even more than "We"—we replace this dangerous development with something simpler and, as it were, more reliable: we confuse the person who apparently masters the central power

* The reader who is accustomed to Freudian language should keep in mind that the phenomenon which we describe as idolatry must not be confused with simple transference in the Freudian sense of the word. In the case of transference the Ego remains in control of the individual's life; only one image from the unconscious emerges, is projected into the outer world, and influences the individual's behavior—which, however, remains egocentric. Idolatry is the abolition of the Ego and the enthronement of a projected image in place of the real Center.

with the real center itself. He who seems to be the channel, or who at least seems to open the channel of power, now is looked upon as the power itself. He is the Great Magician, the Medicine-Man of primitive tribes, the inspired Founder of modern spiritual movements.

Objectively the primordial images, such as the Great Prophet or Leader, the Great Mother or Priestess, and their negative counterparts, the Ogre and the Sorceress, are so close to the center that, during the first half of our individual life as well as during the first half of our racial history, we can scarcely hope to distinguish them sufficiently. By relapsing into a childlike state of mind during our individual crisis we are again exposed to the same danger: the danger of confusing inwardly the real center with a primordial image, and accordingly, of projecting not only the image but, as it were, the image together with the real center, on a person in the outer world.

This person then becomes our "projected Self." We pivot around him like a satellite around its sun. He is "our life"; without him we are nothing; we accept his valuation, his goal, his taste, and, of course, his philosophy. His word is the unquestionable truth, his judgment is absolute, and his will is the will of the universe. He becomes our god.

When we discussed the problems of egocentricity, we had to say that the Ego finally supersedes the real Self in pretended assumption of all the functions of the latter: the Ego replaces the We-group (therefore it cannot love any one else); and it takes the place of God (therefore it has no ethical scruples). Now we find that a similar process takes place if the second half of our Ego-crisis is replaced by a pseudo-conversion. One of the images becomes the representative of the real Self and therefore of the We-group and of God. But this image is not identified with the individual's own personality, it is not called "I"; it is projected into the outer world and identified with a human being who is consequently considered as a super-human entity. This is the psychological essence of idolatry.

The subjective experience of the person who idolizes some one else is "fascination." He is awake and conscious, of course, he can reason and judge—but his viewpoint is completely different from the viewpoint of all other people except of those who are fascinated by the same idol. And it is extremely important to add that the idolater is not egocentric at all. He is idol-centered, but not Ego-centered; and he is, therefore, capable of sacrifice and service. This is why idolaters can be organized into powerful groups, while egocentric people doom every organization to inefficiency. Both, however, the idolater and the Ego-worshipper, serve the wrong center. They represent two different kinds of eccentricity, and therefore both will perish finally from the same disease: their lack of central power which means lack of creativity.

With regard to human history idolatry is even more important than egocentricity. The latter may account for a large part of the evil and suffering in our world; but it is related to individuals, and we know that during the second half of the individual life the power of the Ego decreases. It may do much harm but it will die before it reaches its destructive goals. Idolatry, on the other hand, is related to larger groups (except for the "great love" which is often mutual idolatry between one man and one woman).

And idolatrous groups live longer and are more influential than egocentric individuals. They are able to form pressure groups, religious movements and political parties of considerable importance. And the lifetime of more than one generation may pass before the lack of creativity, which idolatry has in common with egocentricity, finally brings about their collapse.

2. THE IDOLATROUS GROUP

In a superficial estimate we can assume that every individual with an average life-span of sixty years may spend at least one year in a state of critical or even catastrophic inner disturbance. This may be one entire year filled with serious emergencies, dangerous experiences and difficult decisions; or there may be many, let us say six or twelve, such periods spread out irregularly over the sixty years, each lasting a month or two.

In a city of a hundred thousand inhabitants there are at any given moment at least fifteen hundred people (we repeat: normal people, not neurotics) who have lost their inner equilibrium. Their egocentricity is breaking down and they would be able to discover their real center—or better: the power and the glory of the real center would break through the débris of the collapsing Ego like the sun through the clouds—if it were not for the false prophets, the blind leaders of blind men, who create idolatry instead of faith, and advertise a cheap pseudo-center instead of the real treasure which can be bought only by giving up everything else.

During public emergencies such as earthquakes, floods,

epidemics, economic depressions, revolutions and wars, the number of individual crises is multiplied considerably. And in a period of rapid social change as, for instance, when an agricultural country is suddenly industrialized, practically nobody can avoid the inner crisis precipitated by the change of outer circumstances. Then real religion as well as all pseudo-religions have their great opportunity. These are the hot-beds where the decisive historical movements start, where progress or destruction, health or sickness for the coming generation are prepared, and where each individual decides, consciously or unconsciously, whether he will worship an idol and increase darkness, or serve the real center and contribute to the power of light. But none of us can escape entirely the errors of our century. We can only endeavor to be swayed by them as little as possible.

Ministers, doctors, psychologists, counselors, teachers, writers, artists, actors, politicians, newspaper men and movie-producers—all of us, knowingly or unknowingly, participate in the collective guilt of our time: we produce idolatry instead of faith. We exploit the crises of our fellow-men, the breakdown of their egocentricity, their suffering and their opportunity for further development, for our own egocentric or idolatrous goals. We loudly proclaim our philosophy, our art, our policy as the general remedy, and by doing so we—silently—offer ourselves as idols. For most of us, to be a success means to be idolized.

Consciously there may exist a strong antipathy against hero-worship. But much stronger, though less conscious, is our general antipathy against responsible, independent, creative personal development. We like equality, but we confuse it—as long as we are egocentric—with conformity. Our Ego misuses the fact of our human imperfection in order to level or to deny the different degrees of maturity and integration. And when we become idolaters, or idols, the only difference in values which we admit, of course, is based on idolatry: the idol being the only absolute value. In other words, most of us want to remain either egocentric "rugged individualists" and, if possible, idols for others, or enthusiastic idolaters, or peculiar mixtures of both—as long as life allows us to be so. But finally life destroys all eccentricity.

For a certain time, however, the group of idolaters seems to be more immune from the crucial tests of history than the egocentric individual who cannot meet the requirements of creative development. First of all, the members of this group have a good conscience, they are not haunted by feelings of inferiority or insecurity. Their leader knows all the answers, he has solved all the problems, no doubt is left; even if here and there an individual member fails, the group as a whole is perfectly right.

The Ego-center has been dissolved. This is a real advantage, because it effects simultaneously the removal of the Shadow. No fear, no tension, no anxiety spoil the inner welfare of the group members. They are individually happy, carefree and relaxed. They have no personal sorrows. The group will take care of everything. The paradise, indeed the lost paradise of the "Original We-group" which had been destroyed by the "Breach of the

We," is reestablished. The nostalgia of these many years has been fulfilled—and for the moment at least it seems irrelevant whether this wonderful success represents progress or regression; whether the happy group is living in a mediæval state of mind or exploring the possibilities of the future—they do not care, they are happy.

Moreover, they are unanimous, and that gives them a special sense of security. One person could be mistaken. But fifty—or five hundred—cannot be wrong. And then they have realized, all of them, a certain kind of growth. What used to be impossible is done now without difficulty. A man with a serious speech-inhibition has learned to talk; a lady who could not refrain from talking now seems to be the incarnation of modesty. There is some real reintegration, since the Shadow has disappeared and the general consent of the group prevents all malevolent criticism. The new experience of brotherhood brings many buried talents to light. The group seems to be supported by creative power, and the leader seems to be a real prophet.

The Shadow and its disastrous results—tension, inhibition and fear—have been eliminated; but the real center has not been reached. It remains hidden in the unconscious, its creativity stalled and its mask, its outer appearance, projected on the Idol who now represents the center of many individuals and of the group as a whole. This projection is the sham-We-center of a sham-We-group, and it displays an amazing amount of sham-creativity. Finally it creates its own counterpart, the Anti-Idol, and its own destruction.

The individual member of the group has no sorrows,

but the group as a whole has many. The member fears nothing; his philosophy is right, his conscience is clear, his cause will and must succeed in history. The group as such, however, and its leader or its board of executives, face a different picture. There are competitive groups, propagat‧ ing terrible heresies, and they are extremely successful. They have to be fought, conquered, exterminated—or they will annihilate this group which alone is in possession of the full truth.

The Shadow has been removed from the inner structure of the individual; now it emerges anew, multiplied, reinforced and projected into the outer world. Just as the individual Shadow used to be the enemy and the abomination of the Ego, now the rival group, the worshipers of the competitive idol, become the enemies and the abomination of the idolatrous group. The Ego used to transfer the rôle of the adversary, for instance the negative father-image, on different people who subsequently became the substitutes for the original "enemy." Now the group as a whole projects the image of the arch-enemy, that is, a kind of super-enemy or devil, on another group of idolaters and especially, of course, on the other Idol.

The parallelism between the egocentric individual and the idolatrous group can be carried still a step further. The Ego through its one-sidedness originates the Shadow, the center of the repressed functions within the individual's own unconscious structure. Then the same functions and qualities appear in the outer world; the rôle of the enemy is unconsciously transferred to some one else. The "evil" is first located outside the individual; later it is recognized as a part of our inner life; the transference is traced to its source; and this discovery usually initiates the crisis, the breakdown of the Ego, and the start of a new life, either real faith or idolatry.

Exactly the same process can be observed in the development of the idolatrous group. The group first discovers the outer enemy, the rival group and the competitive Idol. This engenders outer danger, fight, discipline and aggressiveness, which constitutes the belligerent or heroic period of the group's history. Rather soon, however, the next step follows, leading in the opposite direction. Consciously the idolater cannot understand how a normal person could possibly worship another Idol than his. His Idol appears (to him) to be the real Self and the center of reality; the others claim the same for their Idol and their vision of life. And the two Idols contradict each other completely. One group, let us say, idolizes the austere, ascetic rules of misunderstood monasticism, their leader wearing a black monk's hood and a long beard; while the other group tries to live in the complete anarchy, promiscuity and irresponsibility of misunderstood "return to nature," its leader wearing nothing but the green vines of Dionysius. To the majority of mankind both groups are equally ridiculous; but in their own eyes they are the only "righteous" people in the world; and to each other they are the arch-enemy and abomination. From the psychological point of view the very fact that they exist together and that they are not able to redeem each other, means that both of them are doomed. Indeed, history often destroys one idolatrous group through another one; but not so much by outer warfare as by an inner process of fermentation.

Consciously the ascetics in our example despise and pity the Dionysians; and vice versa. Both of them enjoy the superiority of having the right insight and the mission with which to convert their opponents. As long as a member of the ascetic group meets the Dionysians officially, nothing will happen. He will preach, arouse resistance, and go away with the deep satisfaction of a martyr for his cause. As soon, however, as he meets them privately he will make the strange and dangerous discovery that, after all, those horrible Dionysians are not quite as bad as they are pictured in the pamphlets of the asceticists. There is some understanding possible; some inner response, some "yes" arises within the visitor's mind where his group loyalty would demand a reckless and blind "No!" The un-lived life of the ascetic is experienced in the Dionysian group; and vice versa.

This discovery prompts a new inner crisis in the visitor. The value of his group, the truth of his idolatry, the identity of his Idol with the real center, are questioned—and all the birth-pangs of the maturing personality begin once more. The second half of his crisis cannot now again be blocked. He relapses out of the sham security of the idolatrous group into the unbearable uncertainty and lone-liness of his private doubts and errors and experiments. Thus he learns the bitter lesson that each individual has to find the way alone, by himself, and that no ready-made formula, no group conviction, no Idol can spare us the hardship of our own development. And by going the way which he is forced to go, he finally finds himself, and the real center, and the real "We."

This individual member is lost to his former group, and his case becomes a temptation and danger to many of his fellow-idolaters. He has lost his faith in the Idol, he has left the group; and the fact that his infidelity, painful as it might have been, did not destroy him, but on the contrary gave him increasing health and creativity—this fact imperils the group and the power of its Idol more seriously than any outer enemy could do.

The spell of the Idol has to be defended by every means. Persuasion and force, praise and punishment, lies and calumnies are used, indeed must be used, with reckless cruelty. Their "highest values of life" are at stake, and since their Idol to them is God, or at least first cousin to God, no bad conscience or feeling of guilt can arise, and "anyone who kills you will imagine that he is performing a service to God." (John 16:2, Moffatt.) This is the source of all fanaticism.

Every idolatrous group is prone to project its unlived group life, its unconscious Anti-Idol or Devil, on its inner enemies, the rebels within its own ranks, even more than on the outer enemy, the rival group or the competitive Idol. Each idolater is imperiled by the potential collapse of the group. Each one is afraid that he may have to face the second half of his private crisis; therefore, in defending his Idol he defends his own immaturity; and in cursing the rebellious infidel he tries to prevent his own relapse into the process of development. Therefore he is as ruthless as a drowning man fighting for his last chance of life.

If the idolater is forced to admit that the Idol does not

solve all the problems, and that there is therefore "un-lived life" in the idolatrous group, he will instantly dis-cover that the group has not solved all his private prob-lems either, and the responsibility for the "unlived life" will shift from a collective to an individual one. He will discover that each member is accountable for the collective debts which the group has accumulated. Consequently the relapse from idolatry into individualism originates terrible feelings of guilt. And the lack of any center or pseudo-center—the Ego having already failed earlier, the Idol failing now, and the real center not yet being available— throws all the members of the collapsing idolatrous group into a state of utmost confusion, and confusion results in anxiety.

The psychological situation at such a moment seems to be rather close to the appalling description of the great tribulations in Matthew 24, when Jesus foretold the de-struction of the Temple and what great calamities would precede it. Many scholars have thought that these descrip-tions were nothing but "old Jewish traditions" which did not fit in with Jesus' teachings nor with reality. Depth-psychology has now rediscovered this phenomenon in the life of individuals as well as of groups and nations. And the microscope of psychology is not even necessary, for wherever we look in history—present and past—we find tribulation; and we begin to understand that this is a way —the more painful of two possible ways—which may lead us upward to a new plane of development. These crises, therefore, have to come; "but the end is not yet."

3. The Idol's Tragedy

The most tragic example of an idolatrous group is a family in which one member is idolized by all the others. Imagine a young mother who loses her husband or feels betrayed by him. Her egocentric hopes break down, her Ego resigns; life would be meaningless to her were it not for her only child. For him, however, she continues her toils; he becomes the center and the justification of her further existence. She has overcome her Ego, her whole life is one of sacrifice and service; but she has not found the real center: she serves an Idol. She gives herself to her son, but she cannot give her son to a cause, or to God. The boy to her is more valuable than anything or any one in the universe, and if God should threaten to take him away she would say: "Thou canst not do this, for it would be immoral, and Thou must remain moral. If the boy dies then I will see, God, that Thou dost not really exist." God has to serve the boy, not the boy, God.

All idolized family members are gradually depraved by the superhuman values which are ascribed to them. They can never measure up to the expectations of their environment and they do not even try to do so. They simply pretend to be, not by endeavor and achievement but by their very birthright, the superhuman being which their worshippers want to see in them. The Idol, in this case, accepts his idolization, he believes in his own godliness. And the result is not—as his mother may hope—a new Christ, but a cruel, reckless oriental despot, who cold-bloodedly annihilates his opponents.

The mother who believes that her child is an angel by this error forces him to become a devil. The husband who idolizes his wife brings about her moral and physical decay. We destroy what we want to preserve most eagerly. The unconscious suicide of the Ego, which we mentioned earlier, is paralleled by the unconscious murder of our idols. But in idolatry the secret crime is more efficient and more far reaching: the idolaters kill their Idol and the Idol kills its worshippers. All evil is busy destroying itself.

In larger groups we often find the same development as in the idolatrous family. "Cæsarean madness" is the typical fate of the human being who confuses himself with God. And the larger the number of worshippers the more people are suddenly faced with the "inner tribulation," namely the second half of their individual crises, when at last the Idol is unmasked as a poor lunatic or a morbid fool. And so strong is our fear of the "inner tribulation" that when our Idols begin to collapse some of us succeed in whitewashing, in repairing them time and again. Or we worship a notorious fool rather than live without our Idol.

If the idolized person honestly believes in his own absolute value and power, he may perform miracles and wield an uncanny spiritual influence over thousands of people, until the unavoidable Cæsarean madness destroys him and turns the enthusiasm of his followers into anxiety and "gnashing of teeth." If the idolized person is aware of his predicament, however, two opposite attitudes are possible. He may be an egocentric and exploit the illusions of his admirers, laughing at their gullibility, as is the case, unfortunately, with many artists, actors and lecturers. Or he may be more or less objective and eager to serve the real center. Then he will strive gradually to open the eyes of his followers and to make them independent of himself as soon as he can. They might do their best to prevent this progress; but, if he really lives out of his center, he will finally force them through darkness and loneliness into maturity. That is what Jesus did. His is one of the very few examples in history which show (in the three temptations) that not only egocentricity but idolatry can be avoided, and that when it arises among the disciples it can be overcome and corrected. It was this he meant, when he said: "My going is for your good. If I do not depart, the Helper will not come to you" (John 16:7, Moffatt). And then by his death he forced them, against their will, to face the last phase of their own crises, to grow fearless and independent and mature, and to be initiated into the life of the Spirit.

Yet there is another tragedy which threatens all idolatrous groups and which can postpone the final collapse of the Idol and the new beginning of spiritual life for an indefinite time. That is the egocentric deviation of idolatry.

The idolaters have to defend their Idols not only against outer enemies (competitive groups) and inner enemies (possible renegades in their midst) but also against their own inner doubts. When they joined the group, as we said before, all problems seemed to be solved, apparently no aspect of life remained unlived, and the Ego together with the Shadow was reintegrated into the new—though eccentric—We-experience. Ten years later, however, the situation is different. The inner life of the individual has grown, and this growth should have been, but was not, a conscious development. The real center has continued to be creative. But the Idol is separated from the real center, denying its existence and pretending to be the center itself. Therefore, the Idol is not creative. Its new contributions to group life are meager and similar to the pseudo-productivity of the Ego: the remnant of power, great or small, but no longer increasing, is spread out thinly; living thoughts are replaced by empty analogies or artificial definitions, and questions which cannot be answered are discarded as being "against the law."

The further growth of the individual member cannot take place inside the conscious life of the group; nor inside his own consciousness, which must not differ from the life of the group. Thus the new development is confined to the unconscious, which means a primitive and elementary awakening of images and this, according to the creed of the group, should not exist at all. Imagine a boy who is "converted" at the age of twelve and becomes a member of the ascetic group which we mentioned before. Good people, he is taught, have no sex life. At the age of twenty-two he still has no conscious sex life, he still is a loyal member of the group. But unconsciously he indulges in wild and sadistic fantasies, and his dreams reveal the sexual level of a caveman. In the opposite case, a girl has joined in the exuberance of her teens the Dionysian group which boasts of its promiscuity. Sexual restrictions, she assumes, are silly; modern people laugh at them. At twenty-

five, however, she begins to feel a peculiar longing for
husband and child; and to stifle her natural growth, her
taste for monogamy, she has to proclaim loudly, in words
and actions, that modern man is polygamous—and shallow
—and disgusted with his shallowness.

In both cases the desperate war against real life is waged
for the sake of a certain kind of sham-life which may be
properly described as the Group-Ego. Its relation to the
real center is similar to the relation of the individual Ego
to the same center. The difference, however, is that the
Group-Ego is a collective mask, expressed in terms of
"We" (*we* are asexual; or, *we* are polygamous); and,
therefore, has more tenacity than the individual Ego. The
relationship between the Group-Ego and the Idol itself
can best be described in terms of development. The Idol at
first is a person. Later he may be superseded by a place,
like a palace or a temple, or by some insignia, like a crown
or a garment. All this, however, does not sufficiently
protect the idolatrous group against the danger of accruing
unlived life. Therefore around the Idol a fortress is built
in the form of habits, rules, laws, theories, and especially
an elaborate educational system.

The philosophers prove, the teachers teach, the lawyers
proclaim and the policemen show by physical force that
the Idol is right. And all this together creates an impersonal style of life which more and more obliterates the
original Idol. The latter, at least, was a person, and deviated as he may have been, he lived a tragic life, deserved
our human interest, and aroused psychological curiosity.
Group-egocentricity, however, is a dead, mechanical ap-

paratus, unconsciously designed to protect the group against its own creativity. If the Idol is the mask of the real center, the Group-Ego can be described as the coffin of this mask, a beautiful whitewashed sepulcher. In literature it appears as a rigid system of ideas, an "Ism."

The characteristics of the "Ism" are the same as those of egocentricity. The first is the assumed completeness of the vision of reality. The "Ists" know, or at least they say, "one day we will know" everything. And facts which disturb their views are boldly denied. The physicist, for instance, if he is an idolatrous Ist, cannot discover any meaning in dreams; nor can the Christian Scientist, if he is an idolatrous Ist, discover the reality of matter. Every Ism in this sense is absolutism; even the relativist believes that his relativism is absolutely right.

Second, the Ism includes, visibly or invisibly, a rigid valuation. He who subscribes to the Ism is good. All others are bad, or at least stupid; they have to be instructed or changed, and if necessary forced to acknowledge the truth. In this sense every Ism is moralism.

Third, the real center is excluded, because the Ism is based on idolatry and the Idol replaces the center. Continuing creation, the essentially new, therefore, cannot be acknowledged (lest it overthrow the Idol and his Ism). It is instructive to see how the opposite Isms have solved this problem in similar ways. Natural "scientism" says that by means of cause and effect the future is determined, nothing really new can happen, the parts of every new whole have been present from the beginning. And the "theologist" says God once created the universe; now he supports it; but there is no new creation any more. In both cases the Group-Ego is protected against dangerous surprises—theoretically. Practically, however, the growing though repressed life will rebel against its imprisonment. It will bring about one explosion after another until the Isms themselves are exploded.

The Ism defends itself, asserting eagerly how and why all other Isms are wrong. But it has no adequate weapons against real growth. And one day life will present it with undeniable facts which simply show that the Ism is insufficient. (Thus the telescope proved that the Ptolemaic view of the world was wrong; and hypnotism proved that materialism was inadequate.) But, curiously enough, for large numbers of people the authority of the Ism, or the Idol which supports it, is strong enough to outweigh the most obvious facts—until the breakdown of the corresponding social patterns prompts the inner crisis by outer disaster.

This process is hastened by the fact that more and more egocentric individuals misuse the same Ism together with the idolaters. The Idol is inaccessible for egocentric people, but the Group-Ego can be exploited by them. Many Ists therefore have not only to face the second half of their crisis but the first half too. That means that all their private egocentric blunders, tricks and even crimes are committed "in the name of the Ism." And this, fortunately, though unjustly, promotes the catastrophe.

All great religions are eruptions of truth. Christianity in particular shows an inexhaustible power, which time and again has exploded the Group-Egos of deviated communities as often as they became too rigid. And its dynamics seem to increase rather than to diminish. Idolatry and group-egocentricity can throw their poisonous cloak over everything; all sciences and arts, philosophies and religions can be misused in the service of the Group-Ego as well as of the private Ego. And every prophet can be misunderstood as an Idol. If they lose their power, smothered by the Ego-love of their followers, they will disappear. It is the most encouraging fact in history that Christianity, however often and deeply it has been misused and misunderstood, has never been quenched nor lost its spiritual power.

VII

CONSCIOUS GROWTH

1. INDIVIDUATION

Our feud against egocentricity is sometimes misinterpreted as a disparagement of individualism. However, it is a fact we observe everywhere that people who try to live for their own sake, considering the satisfaction of their private desires as their highest goal, are disowned by life in an unmistakable way. They are doomed to tension, frustration, irritability and fear, though the latter may remain unconscious for a long time. Therefore, we want to avoid or decrease as much as we can this deviation which we have carefully investigated and labelled "egocentricity." It is similar to, but more refined than, egoism and almost identical with what is usually called "rugged individualism." But we do not condemn individualism as such.

All human life begins in a peculiar state of instinctive collectivity, which psychologically may be described as "the original We-experience." The little child, like the primitive savage, has no consciousness of being different from other members of the group. Subjectively he is not aware of any conflict between his own interest and the interest of the others. And objectively he shows no difference between the conscious and unconscious strata of his mind. We describe his psychological state as "tribal consciousness." The individual knows, feels, thinks and wants only what the group knows, feels, thinks and wants. All mental and emotional forces, courage and fear, joy and sorrow, belong to the group and not to the individual. The little child has to share his life with others, or it cannot develop.—This organic unity of the original We-group is beautiful, but not enviable.

The way of history has been, and as far as we know, the goal of history still is, the unfolding of human life and especially the gradual evolution from tribal to individual consciousness, and from collective to personal responsibility. Unfolding, "differentiation," however, has to be balanced by unification or "integration": the individual should become conscious not only of his unique personality (for every one is unique and cannot be replaced by any one else) but he should become conscious also of his own membership in the group and of his responsibility for the other members and for the group as a whole. His consciousness should become personal, he should discover that he is different, with special qualities and rights and duties of his own, but his consciousness should not be narrowed down to the interests of one single individual. It should not even remain tribal, in the sense of understanding the qualities, needs and interests of the group. It should grow, include and integrate the qualities, needs and interests of other groups: it should become universal. Our consciousness becomes more personal, different from other consciousnesses, and at the same time more universal: we become alive to our participation in the development of mankind, we become world-conscious. But each individual should find and maintain his own viewpoint, his own individual kind of world-consciousness. There should be no uniformity; nor should there be indistinctness, nor indulgence in vague generalities.

The word consciousness, however, denotes only one important aspect of our human problems. The other aspect, equally important, and inseparable from the first, may be characterized by the word "power." Growing consciousness without growing power is a miserable deformity. The clairvoyant who does not know what to do with his insight is a frequent example. If his consciousness were really clear he would know that he has to dig up and develop his power, courage and aggressiveness until they equal his clairvoyance. Then he would become what he was meant to be: one of the superior strategists of human evolution. And in the opposite case, the person who wields more power than consciousness is a dangerous maniac. He is almost bound to become an idol. People will admire him and expect him to be as wise as he is strong, and soon he will break down under the responsibilities which life bestows on him far beyond his conscious horizon.

Thus we may say: The equilibrium of consciousness and power constitutes the desirable type of character which history, as far as we know, wants us and almost compels us to develop. We call this type the mature personality, and the process of maturing which leads up to this goal, individuation. In order to understand the latter term more clearly, however, two questions must be answered which necessarily arise from the foregoing discussion.

The first question is a very old one: How can the individual, becoming more and more conscious of his individual needs, possibilities, and desires, at the same time serve the group and its interest? Is there not a fundamental conflict between social duties and personal enjoyment? Were not the moralists right in decreeing that the individual must be compelled by laws, praise and punishment to fulfill his duties towards society, and that otherwise there would be anarchy and social chaos?

The second question is a new one. Fifty years ago it could not yet have been asked, because it presupposes the knowledge and acknowledgment of conscious and unconscious psychological functions. The question is twofold, related to consciousness and power: If individuation means that the individual emerges out of the tribal consciousness, is it not then advisable for the individual to separate himself from his tribe as much as possible? How can he feel responsible for the group, and how can he maintain his membership in the group though he seeks to free himself from it more and more? And if the power at first is concomitant with tribal consciousness, must not the individual consciousness lose all power? Or, how can the power be shifted from the tribe to the individual? How can tribal power be transformed into personal power?

The answer to both questions is one. Based on our theory concerning the structure of the human mind, it represents a working hypothesis, scientifically neither better nor worse than other hypotheses. It has the advantage of being largely in accordance with the experiences of many centuries as recorded in religious literature, and it can be used and tested by any one who wishes to do so.

The answer is this: Our duties towards ourselves and towards our social environment coincide. Indeed there is only one duty, namely: to grow mature. To find ourselves, our center, our highest value, means to find our group, our spiritual home and our positive relationship to God. It means unlimited growth, both of individual creativity and of expanding brotherhood.—The pessimist objects: This is a beautiful fairy tale, well suited to win acquiescence, but it does not solve our problems because it is not true.

Answer: It holds good in practical life. Only our egocentric goals are in conflict with our social duties—and with our duties towards ourselves—and ultimately with our egocentric interests. Even from the viewpoint of the Ego it would be better to be less egocentric. But the real interest, the natural goal and the ethical duty of the individual, is to become aware of his real nature so that by expanding his consciousness he discovers his inner imagery, representing his fellow-men.

Both his inner images and his companions in outer life are reciprocal factors in his development; in hurting them he hurts himself. He has membership in many groups; and the more richly his inner imagery unfolds itself the larger grows the number of individuals, and groups, and groups of groups whom he understands and loves. His responsibility for other people is the same as his responsibility for his eye or his hand; what happens to them happens to his inner image, and that means to the organs of his mental organism. If he does not develop his capacity to love his fellow-men, the inner images will atrophy, the buried talents will degenerate and grow like cancer; he will hate his brothers; and his unlived life, the psychic cancer, will torture him until he stops and turns to face his crisis—or until he dies.

The egocentric person, the immature individual, disappears. He perishes or he outgrows his handicaps. And the same is true for idolaters and egocentric groups. In the long run human history is an endless series of inexorable ultimata, always handing down the same verdict: grow up or perish. To grow up, however, means to become oneself and that means to become an epitome of mankind, namely to become conscious of human nature—through the images. Or in other words: mankind, through these images, becomes conscious reality within the individual.

Here we reach the point where the deepest riddle of psychology has to be faced. It is the mystery which is indicated in our central equation: the real center, the Self of the individual, is identical with the center of the group and with our relationship to God; or in a simplified formula:

$$\text{The Self} = \text{the We} = \text{He}$$

The Gospel of St. John expresses the same idea in the words ". . . that they may be one, even as we are one— I in them and thou in me—that they may be made perfectly one" (John 17:22-23, Moffatt). Thus the mature personality is on the one hand free, independent and self-responsible; he represents his group and the whole of humanity in his own unique way, and makes his special contribution in his own manner—that is individualism.

And on the other hand he remains and indeed becomes more and more an essential part of the whole. The more his maturity develops the more he sees how dependent he is. His interests and endeavor are concerned with the whole which supports him; the growing brotherhood conditions his inner life; and last but not least, his creative power is the power of the group—it is a super-individual power.

In the mature personality mankind reaches a higher level of consciousness; creation continues, the race, as it were, awakens; deeper and more powerful layers of the collective unconscious are brought to light. They become individualized and remain universal at the same time. Thousands of people find their own problems expressed, lived and solved in the lives and works of these men. The consciousness and the power of the integrated person are at the same time individual and collective. We can find this in variant degrees wherever there are mature people; and it becomes evident beyond doubt when the great names of mankind are mentioned: Dante, Shakespeare, Dostoievsky, Goethe, Beethoven, Lincoln—they are symbols, not idols, of human evolution. (The better we know their deficiencies the less we can idolize them.)

Thus we may say: individuation is the way of human development which leads from tribal power and consciousness to individual power and consciousness by way of growing integration. The collective problems, possibilities and responsibilities become parts of our individual consciousness and tasks for our individual creative power. The sorrows of humanity become our personal sorrows and the creative power of the race is entrusted to us in individual forms.

But the riddle remains. Just how the original center, the tribal or group center, which evidently is one, can be multiplied into innumerable individual centers; and how the different consciousnesses of several individuals are able to preserve their original oneness, or regain it after having lost it through differentiation—this problem cannot be solved by philosophical discussions. And it is useless to make lofty metaphysical statements to the effect that beyond space and time there is neither oneness nor multiplicity nor number. We ourselves simply have to live, to grow, and to mature. Only in this way can we come nearer to the truth.

One consideration, however, concerning the relationship of consciousness and power, may throw some additional light on the course we must follow. There are two kinds of consciousness. You can be conscious of your hand as you are conscious of a tree: the object exists in the outer world and you can study it from outside. Now close your eyes and be conscious of your hand from inside, and you will discover that you are within your hand. The hand is you. If someone hits it you say, "You hit *me*." Then, look at your wife, first from the outside: she is an object, like the tree; second from inside: try to feel her existence as you felt your hand. If some one hurts her you will feel, "He hurts *me*"; and the more so the more your contact image, the Eve image, is alive. If you don't feel it then do something to overcome your egocentricity or idolatry.

The inner kind of consciousness—we may call it subjec-

tive consciousness—is identical with power. If some one
steps on your toes you will react vigorously, and if he
hurts your wife, your Eve-image will tell you immediately what has to be done. No lack of courage, no alibi, no
"reasonable scruples" will stop you; your power will be
aroused and will act.—Otherwise you are cut off from
your Eve-image by egocentricity or by idolatry.

Expanding consciousness includes both the subjective
and the objective attitudes. We develop our objective consciousness by seeing and understanding the outer world
more completely. Here the inner imagery provides the
organs of perception. You cannot perceive what happens
to an underprivileged child unless you harbor a responsive
image of boy or girl. Yet if you do so you cannot limit
yourself to objective observation. You cannot help being
involved emotionally, subjectively, centrally, and that
means religiously. Here again the inner images function as
channels of power. What happens to the underprivileged
children happens to you. They are hurt, your inner images
suffer with them, your creative power is challenged. You
will react vigorously, provided you are not petrified by
egocentricity or idolatry.

The relationship between power and consciousness is
dynamic. It forces us to grow or to suffer. We may describe it in the following way: "I am hurt because the underprivileged child is hurt. I am furious, I am a channel of
subjective power. At the same time I look more objectively at the one who hurts the child. And I feel with
him, too. I become subjectively conscious of him; he, too,
is represented in my inner imagery. I understand him, he

is part of myself. I hurt the child when he does it. I hurt myself. My reaction against him becomes reaction against myself. If I hurt him, I hurt myself anew. The outer conflict becomes an inner one. I have to create a new way of dealing with both of them, or they will destroy my life. I must be, and will be, creative."

Expanding consciousness is identical with expanding creative power, or it is not expanding at all. And if it expands it brings about a deeper individual responsibility, higher capacities and increasing courage. The creative center is alive, the collective images grow; and both the central power and the images through which it functions become more conscious every day. Thus the mature personality through his own development shows his fellowmen the path to the future. He is the pioneer exploring the next step in evolution. By doing so he furthers creation; and that means he is a servant of God.

2. The Past and the Future

The way of individuation is painful. We can avoid some, but not all, of its suffering by way of prevention through better education, re-education and self-education. And it is here more than anywhere else, in the field of "watching and praying" that religion, psychology and medicine should cooperate. But there will still be crises and catastrophes, with bewilderment, fear and anxiety, even for the best prepared and wisest men. Our own death or the death of our beloved ones may be the crucial test. And if we are able to face this, perhaps we will have to go through the breakdown of the cultural values in our group and our nation. Would we under such circumstances still retain our faith and creativity? Would we be able to go the way of Job?

Theoretically we may say that all suffering is due to deviation. If mankind had never gone astray, if neither Egos nor Idols had replaced the real center, the whole way from tribal to individual consciousness and from the tribe's responsibility for the tribe to the individual's responsibility for the world, would have taken place without fear or suffering. But this is a purely theoretical idea. As a matter of fact every step forward in the development of individuals and groups is hampered by fears and sorrows, prejudices and inhibitions, consciously as well as unconsciously, and individually as well as collectively.

Our inner evil, the disease which thwarts our development and confuses our history is simple in its direction: it is rebellion against time, as we have stated above, and therefore is resistance against evolution, or, if we prefer the religious term, against creation itself. Yet it is complicated in its inner structure and cannot be overcome by the simple and childlike resolve "not to sin any more." We must study it carefully and overcome it gradually by wise and long-range religious strategy.—It is in this area that depth-psychology can and will make its contribution.

Our general aversion against time and what time does to us results in the conviction that we are completely conditioned by the past. The past, we think, is certain, we can rely on it, while the future is insecure and dangerous. We try to build dams and canals to control the floods of the future. We "take thought," we trouble about what we are to eat or drink, applying our experiences, conscious and unconscious, to the future, as if circumstances ten years from now would still be the same as they were ten years ago. That is why we "store up treasures where moth and rust corrode" and cherish our egocentric prejudices as if they were truths.

In the realm of mental life a false conviction becomes a mock-truth, an illusion. It bears fruit as a psychic reality; it causes reactions of infinite consequence. And as an error it leads finally to catastrophe. Thus the conviction that the past is more important and more real than the future influences our thinking in science and philosophy to the effect that causality and its correlative ideas, determinism and irresponsibility, are considered as the exclusive scientific truth. The opposite view, creativity, freedom and responsibility, is deemed poetical dreaming and idealistic superstition.

This false conviction about the past, however, does not originate in the lofty realm of thought and theory. Its foundations are not to be found in the conscious mind (otherwise philosophical discussion would lead us nearer to truth, which it never does). A wrong philosophy is always based on some distortion in the unconscious structure of the philosopher's mind. Discouragement of little children engenders unconscious fears and inhibitions which later produce, unconsciously, the wrong kind of thinking, thinking based on real experiences and true facts but wrongly interpreted.

It is not our conscious philosophy, our "reasonable caution," it is our unconscious discouragement and its result, our inner "eccentricity," which force us to rely on the past and to forestall the future. There are in the first line, of course, our individual experiences, some of them still in our memory, most of them forgotten or repressed. We have learned that we must not do certain things and that certain other things must be done; we have learned to pigeonhole people and situations: "this is good, that is bad; this man is kind, the other one is dangerous." The world has become a rigid pattern of categories. And worst of all, we think we know ourselves; we mistake our capacities and limitations in such a way that actually we are limited by our belief in our limitations, and yet are incapable in spite of the confidence in our capacities. Egocentric confidence does not help us, and objective confidence is not available as long as we trust only the past. In this sense we are determined, unfree, conditioned; we are slaves of the past; we are discouraged, limited, inhibited; and the best thing that the future could bring us is a terrible crisis.—And as you know, old slaves prefer to remain slaves.

Are we not right in smiling condescendingly at our children's undaunted hope for a golden time to come? "They are not yet disillusioned, not yet sobered down by reality," we think. And most of us cannot imagine that there could be a third point of view, fusing the confidence of the child and the disillusionment of the adult into real courage and real faith.

But the discovery of a third point is a complicated task. Not only do our individual negative experiences have to be overcome; we are not only liable for our own mistakes; we have to pay, as it were, the debts of our parents, our century and our whole race. The "breach of the original We" and all the ensuing discouragements of our childhood were possible only because our parents and educators were not creative enough. Their love lacked either wisdom or warmth. And this was so because they themselves had not been brought up in the right way. Their faults were the results of the faults of their educators; and so back to Adam's fall. We are saturated with the results of the egocentricity or idolatry of all our ancestors. The transmission of evil from one generation to the other has been described in Chapter Two, Part Two: we may call this method of transmission the outer or educational way. Yet there is an inner means too by which negativity is transferred from one generation to the other: this may be called the biological way. And here is the point at which we need the collaboration of natural scientists, physicians, and especially endocrinologists.

The genes, as we know, carry the human inheritance, physical as well as psychological, and transmit all kinds of destructive and degenerative factors as well as positive ones. Concerning the inheritance of inner images very little is known. A certain difference between the imagery of far distant races seems to exist, constituting at the same time the cause and effect of the cultural background. Within the deeper layers of the minds of half-castes our psychological research reveals not two different sets of images, but two styles or atmospheres which make the images much richer, more varied and less distinct (but not less rigid) than in the case of pure racial stock. The son

of a Slavic father and a French mother after having sufficiently analyzed his "unconscious of the past" was able to
distinguish rather exactly the two possibilities or styles of
life equally at his disposal. He amused himself by pre-
ferring one year what he called his "Tolstoi-soul" and the
next year his "Anatole-France-soul." Thus far he was not
a slave of his past.

More important for us is the psychological inheritance
which is concomitant with the slighter degrees of "blas-
tophthoria," that is, the damage done to the genes by alcoholism, syphilis or psychotic tendencies. If one of your
four great-grandfathers was a drinker, to a slightly greater
degree than the average of his contemporaries, or if one of
your ancestors was a great musician or a very secluded
misanthrope—you will surely have to pay the price for
what they did or omitted to do. Is it your glandular system which influences your imagery? Or do the inner
images cause the glands to work the wrong way? In any
case, your inheritance prompts you to react more violently
to all negative experiences which challenge your nervous
equilibrium. If the teacher blames you, you feel hellfire
and brimstone raining down upon your head, while your
classmate in the same situation can scarcely refrain from
laughing. Later you are driven to write novels or to found
a new denomination, while he lives comfortably by selling
insurance. The "sins of our fathers" are alive within
us; we have to redeem our ancestry or we cannot live at
all.

Another chain of cause and effect must be mentioned
here, too. It is not necessarily "unconscious" in the proper

sense of the word; it may be recorded in documents, letters and family tradition. You may know it, yet you have to pay for it, to accept it as part of your personal fate, and to forgive your ancestors for having acted as they did. This is the fact that one of them, let us say, about 1700, migrated to Russia, or to America. Another one married the wealthiest girl of Boston; or he could have done so and married a Gypsy instead. The third one held many shares of a deserted gold mine and sold them the day before the mine turned out to be the richest one in the country.—Our financial and social situation is largely conditioned by our forefathers' decisions and actions; and we have to accept them as though we had made them ourselves.

Our responsibilities, debts and liabilities are collective and cover the whole of human history. Our nightmares and our sleeplessness, our fear of the future and our hatred of competitors may well be induced or intensified by the gloomy tragedies which our ancestors endured for thousands of years. How can we, discouraged and loaded with negativity as we are, make up for all the accumulated evil of the past? Are we not truly in a debtor's jail?

For twenty or thirty years it looked as though depth-psychology would find the way out. Freudianism and Adlerianism proclaimed the remission of all debts. Bad conscience, feelings of guilt, fear and anxiety were "nothing but" errors acquired in early childhood, and individual repressions resulting from these errors. Two bloody world wars were needed to prove that this was only half of the truth.

Now we know better: Jung discovered the collective

beneath the individual unconscious; and the darkness that we have to face grew to super-human proportions. The more the "unconscious of the past," the storehouse of racial memories, was investigated, the more it seemed to deter-- mine our future. We became more and more enslaved by the past. There was no doubt: depth-psychology, together with medicine, mental hygiene and eugenics were not suffi- cient. Strong as they were they were not strong enough to pay our debts, to free us from our obligations and to open the way to the future.—Then we understood that only religion was able to do this.

And there were religious voices—or were they pseudo- religious ones? Indeed they had been heard already for some time, saying: "There is no evil! Look for the positive value which is to be found within every one and every- thing. Do not countenance negative thoughts or feelings, they are wrong. Everything is beautiful. We are not fet- tered by the past, nor by sin, nor by diseases, nor by wrong social orders. There is no darkness; just believe in the light." It was a powerful message; and it seemed to work. Many people became much happier.

But—cities were raided, thousands of women and chil- dren were maimed . . . "Everything is beautiful, there is no darkness" . . . Millions of soldiers were killed in action, nations reduced nations to starvation . . . "We are not fettered by sin" . . . Are we not? Is there no evil in our world? Should we not do something about it?

Religion without a thorough study of sin, religion with- out awareness of conscious and unconscious, individual and collective darkness, evil and deviation, is not religion but blind idolatry. Let us be aware, as honestly and objectively as we can, of our dangers and negativities. Let us bring to consciousness this terrible "unconscious of the past," let us face the task as depth-psychology reveals it. Let us acknowledge our individual and collective debts. —And, knowing that there is no other possibility, let us look for the really religious way out.—This is what we know about the way out:

During the second half of the crisis both idolatry and egocentricity disappear. Our method of thinking changes completely, not because some one convinces us of a new truth, but because the underlying structure of our mind breaks down and is replaced by a new one which is at the same time old and original. Life once more pivots around the real center as it used to do at the time of tribal consciousness. But during the period of egocentricity our consciousness has been individualized, and now it remains individual. Thus the result is individual consciousness of the real, and that means universal, center. This new-old structure produces a new-old kind of thinking. Gradually our whole vision of life is revised; our emotional attitude towards people and circumstances is transformed; the scope of our consciousness is enlarged; and our responsibility is felt in a new and more comprehensive way.

The change is neither sudden nor complete. It covers several years as a process of organic growth; otherwise the human mind could not stand it. But in a psychological description it is advisable to omit the factor of slow development and to contrast the attitudes and especially the methods of thinking before and after a person's crisis— let us say, for example, at the ages of thirty-five and forty-five, assuming that the crisis reached its climax at the age of forty. And still another preliminary remark is necessary before we enter into this decisive aspect of our psychology. People who have gone through their crises will recognize the facts immediately, even though they may prefer another terminology or even another viewpoint for the description. Those who have made at least a few successful steps through the first stages of the crisis will understand without too much difficulty. But all those who have not yet faced their crises or who have withdrawn from them into idolatry or more sophisticated egocentricity, will not be able to find the slightest degree of meaning in all this. They will say, "Why should we read this stuff? After all, we are not morons!" And they will be right, they should not read it.

Here our psychology is in the same predicament as the preaching of St. Paul because we have to speak about the same paradoxical truth. It is and must be "sheer folly" to most psychologists (I Cor. 1:21-23, Moffatt). But if there are people who have—more or less—gone through this inner change which we call the crisis; and if their experiences and reactions are different from the experiences and reactions of people who have not yet gone so far; then there must be a psychology of "post-critical" life, though "pre-critical" readers will be deaf to its language. Youngsters before they go through puberty cannot appreciate the psychology of married life. The materialist must deem St. Francis a fool. This fact, however, should not prevent our writing on the psychology of St. Francis, provided we can find a viewpoint which allows us to understand his experience.

The change, as we said, expressed itself most clearly in our ways of thinking, in philosophical and scientific reflections as well as in practical considerations. The connection of cause and effect, resulting in concepts of necessity and lack of freedom, is not forgotten, but is embraced in the larger scheme of means and goals. Causality becomes a servant of creative freedom.

The new viewpoint, however, is quite different from the cheap anthropomorphic "teleology" of the year 1600. It is based on carefully observed psychological facts. And it shows in many practical experiences that we are conditioned by the past only in so far as our inheritance provides certain means, limitations and tasks. Our goals and possibilities, our incentive, power and creativity come to us from the future. The past, we may say, limits some of our means, though not all of them; but the future creates new possibilities. We have no wings because our ancestors, millions of years ago, became mammals rather than birds; yet we may build airplanes and fly nevertheless.

The chain of cause and effect is infinite, and so is the pyramid of means and goals. There is no "first cause" and no "final goal." Every goal becomes a means in the service of a still higher goal. And every means can be replaced by another one. This dizzying view should set us free from fear and enable us to play our part in the work of creation in spite of all our handicaps and all our sense of guilt—if only we could find the faith which reveals within ourselves the creative force of the Center. But in the beginning this force is unconscious, unknown, unbelievable, even though it makes us grow and think and act, and sometimes gives us creative ideas long before we overcome egocentricity and idolatry.

Every one, of course, acknowledges that children are conditioned by their own future in so far as they are under the necessity of growing up. In due course they will be adolescents, adults, and finally old people; this much we can foresee. And therefore this development seems to bear out the argument for causality and determinism. The determinist says: "The seed is determined by the parental plant, and likewise the child by his race. He has to grow and to die; his so-called goals are merely biological causes projected into the future; the real causes are to be found in the genes."—Are they, really?—Or is all this only an artificial argument, a round-about way of forcing future-conditioned creatures back into the pattern of past-conditioned dead things?

Determinism and egocentricity are inseparable. As soon as an egocentric person tries to imagine that human evolution may be conditioned by the future he instantly thinks: "Then we are determined by Providence—or by Platonic Ideas, which control reality as lifeless everlasting patterns." Wherever he looks he sees determinism. His Ego needs this view and will defend it to the last, and believe it even when it cannot be defended any more. The following argument, therefore, is not meant as an attempt to convert opponents. It may, however, be an important aid to those who are close to or are already in their crises and who try to free themselves from their own deterministic prejudices.

Children, we said, may be bound to develop in certain

ways and patterns, in so far as they have to repeat—not exactly but more or less—the development of their race. Yet they reach one day the end of the road which, as it were, has been built by their ancestry. They enter the firing line of civilization and have to go ahead alone into the unknown. To what extent are they still determined by the past when they enter the no-man's-land of the future?

As an example think of the problems of marriage. A hundred years ago marriage was a conventional thing; people knew what they were expected to do and they did it. Marriage, then, was a pattern almost entirely conditioned by the past. Now it is different. Every married couple nowadays has to grope its way through a pathless primeval forest. Marriage at this moment is beyond the frontiers of traditional civilization. We know that our children will marry but we do not know how they will do it; and we cannot teach them what they should do. There are books and maps and even agencies pretending to know all about the new country. But at best all they know is the past. They draw conclusions honestly and scientifically, and their conclusions would be right—if life were not changing every day and calling for real creativity, which means travelling without a map and without security.

Every individual in our time has to face situations where not only the outer tradition but even the inner equipment, habits, patterns, instincts and reflexes, fail him completely. What will his answer be if life asks him a new, and hitherto unheard of, question? If he were determined by the past, his inner pattern would produce the answer, but it does not. He is at a loss, forsaken, and he will perish unless something new, unexpected and creative turns up and solves the problem. Where does the new idea come from? Is it a mechanical and necessary result of existing conditions? Then: Why all the birth-pangs of the creative action? And why must some people fail while others succeed and shape the future with their new discoveries?

Fortunately, we have now the means to explore to a certain extent what happens in our unconscious mind during the time of crisis and the ensuing period of creativity. The animal instinct, as we have seen, is in human life largely replaced by collective imagery. The more a given predicament develops into a crisis the more we see the images "regress" to earlier stages. That means the influence of egocentricity and idolatry is undone: the images lose their distortions and their rigidity, they become more primitive and more powerful; or, we may say, they free themselves from the tyranny of idol or Ego and reestablish their original relation to the real center. Then a new development of differentiation and integration begins, the new growth leading to a new kind of life at a higher level of consciousness.

As an example, the case of a young married couple, probably one of the typical cases of our time, may be described in fuller detail. In the interest of discretion, however, it has to be slightly altered, and in order to be clear it will be somewhat simplified.

When the young man fell in love with his prospective wife he went through the first part of his crisis quickly and courageously. Not understanding what happened to him, he nevertheless sensed that some positive development had taken place, changing him "from a boy into a man"; and he knew that he owed this painful and beautiful experience to his bride. Neither Tristan nor Romeo, he felt, could have realized a deeper or more powerful love.

The girl was somewhat less enthusiastic and probably more mature than the boy. She went into the adventure with thoughtful honesty and overcame the resistance of her family without too much trouble. She wanted him to be the father of her children, and her determination gave her courage and—as her aunts and uncles observed—a new kind of beauty. Thus, on their wedding day every one was convinced that they would be a happy household, far above the average.

Three years later, at the climax of their difficulties, they tried to understand the situation psychologically. And what they finally discovered was this: he had developed very early two opposite Eve images, one being an almost exact portrait of his mother (as he saw her, and as she tried to be, hiding all her human deficiencies and all negative emotions). This mother ideal did not know the word "no." She pampered and spoiled the boy, her only child, and handed over all problems of discipline and authority to her husband. The opposite type was represented by an old, though extremely vital, Mexican woman who lived in the neighborhood and who was apparently fond of music and alcohol. This image, which may be called "the gypsy-mother," was despised, forgotten, almost repressed, and recurred only in some strangely exciting anxiety dreams.

Later on the image of the good mother was developed into two new opposites: first a radiant madonna, aloof, blameless, and beautiful like a statue on a golden pedestal; and, second, a kind and motherly nurse who carried all the tenderness and warmth of the earlier "ideal mother." This pre-puberty development resulted from sexual fantasies and daydreams which could not be applied to the former good mother. In the daydreams the nurse then developed into a good-natured sensual creature, half priestess, half prostitute, who without doubt had inherited some traits from the bad Mexican woman. She was well suited to fulfill all the changing desires of the growing boy, but she was so far removed from reality that she caused much feeling of embarrassment and almost of guilt. She was in danger of being condemned and repressed into the unconscious, together with her older sister, the Mexican.

Then the boy met his future wife. Up to this point all girls had been to him either madonnas or nurses. He had either adored them or had enticed them to indulge his insatiable thirst for caresses. Now he found a madonna who was a nurse. She knew how to caress without losing her heavenly dignity. She was motherly, kind, gay and not at all prudish. Thus the two images, madonna and nurse, coincided in the boy's half-conscious mind, and their fusion brought about the change in his character which we have mentioned. This was the first half of his crisis; and he mistook the half for the whole, and increasing strength for increasing maturity. The earlier "good mother" image had been restored, and he did not know that the gypsy-mother was still imprisoned in his unconscious and that her powerful image absorbed the better part of his masculinity.

His wife had learned in early childhood to defend herself against two older brothers and had become a tomboy. But from a few good experiences with her father, who died rather early, she sensed vaguely that one day a man would be able to help her overcome her tomboy attitude and to become her feminine self. During her teens she dominated the boys of her own age and revered some older gentlemen. But the boys left her alone and the older men were of no help to her. She experienced many disappointments and her rigid Ego-pattern was considerably softened. Then she met her future husband and instantly fell in love with him.

He was of her own age but she felt little inclination to dominate him. Instead of the brother image she transferred on him the father image, and for the first time in her life she was docile and tender towards a man who was not twenty years her senior. This new experience made her happy and convinced her that this boy could help her to become a real woman. He expected her to be his "good mother," at once nurse and madonna, and to spoil him without reward. She expected him to take care of her inner development and to overcome her childish tomboy resistance. Thus both of them were conditioned by "the unconscious of the past." Their ideas about the future, their goals and hopes were necessary results of former experiences. They were in the debtor's jail and had to pay for their own and their ancestors' deviations.

The two transferences clashed. Both were bitterly disappointed. Their hopes broke down and their confidence in life and in each other was replaced by dreary pessimism. He developed temper tantrums because she did not caress him as the mother image prescribed; and she became the tomboy again, and a furious one, because he could not awaken the gentle Sleeping Beauty who waited day and night for the daring Prince. Finally they separated; and that was the beginning of the decisive crisis for both of them.

The husband's Ego was identified with the image of "the little one who has to be nursed." Now the nurse failed him; and the breach of the egocentric sham-We was as tragic as the breach of the original We. The Ego, unable to exist without its counterpart, broke down. Sleeplessness, despair and plans of suicide followed. He behaved like a new-born baby without his mother, complaining senselessly, accusing everything and everybody, and doing nothing to change the situation. The regression to earlier attitudes was evident.

The older images turned up; older both individually and racially. The "Mexican woman," the representative of reckless Dionysian power, came to life again. The young man began to drink and to rave. Then he had an accident and was for three days in a hospital. And during this time he realized the state of complete loneliness and darkness which is significant for the climax of our crisis. Forsaken by men, not aware of God, deprived of all values of his former life and of all hopes for the future, he had to face the fact that human life has no right, no claim and no power of its own. And he accepted the fact because it was reality, and reality was nothing but this.

After a long time, presumably several hours, of dullness and vague sensations (at least vague in recollection), of anxiety and nothingness, extreme cold and extreme heat, he awoke to a new and astonishing experience of objectivity. He still felt weak and exhausted, but quite comfortable. Everything seemed to have more vivid color; people were more "real" to him than they used to be; and he realized a peculiar kind of relationship to everything and everybody. He described it as: "a sincere interest but at the same time a serene detachment."

Psychologically we understand that from the viewpoint of his Ego he used to consider everything only with regard to its usefulness or injuriousness to his personal goals. Thus we may say, objects showed him only two colors: white if they pleased his Ego, and black if they offended it. When his egocentricity was replaced, more or less, by objectivity he discovered that they had colors of their own, regardless of their values for him. For the first time, as it were, he saw red and blue and green—the beauty of life. Music could be beautiful though it disturbed his sleep. The nurse was an interesting person, though she did not spoil him at all.

Then the young man thought of his wife. For the first time he discovered her beauty and her personality, apart from her relationship with him. He understood that she had problems, needs and conditions of her own; he saw that he could and should help her; and he remembered some happy moments when, by chance, he had done something important for her development, though he had meant it in the interest of his Ego. Thus he knew that he had the power to make her happy. And suddenly he discovered that he was in love with this "lonely and disappointed creature who looked so desperate and weak, but who was as beautiful and powerful as nature herself."

This latter expression seems to indicate that his inner Eve-image was no longer projected on his wife (which would have meant idolatry) but was used as a means of contact and understanding, directing his own central power, his love, in the right direction. He considered her deficiencies and needs as they actually were instead of imposing on her his arbitrary ideas; and therefore he knew what he had to do. He wrote her a letter which, as she later confessed, was altogether unusual and at once convinced her that he had changed. She felt that he loved her and that she could now trust him. Her Ego and her pride still advised her to be cautious, but she could not help calling him up. Eve responded because Adam was wooing in the right way. The result was a new beginning, new love, and the attempt to develop a new form of marital life with more mutual consideration, understanding and consciousness.

Before his crisis the young man had been largely conditioned by "the unconscious of the past." The first half of his crisis had replaced the more differentiated images (madonna and nurse) by the more primitive image of the ideal mother. This regression however was not sufficient. The egocentric rigidity of the mother image did not allow a practical adjustment to the given situation. He was still unconsciously conditioned by the past. He was still kept, because of his collective debts, in the prison of his ego-centricity. His poor wife, whom he expected to play the rôle of the ideal mother, preferred to run away. He broke down and his regression continued; the counterpart of the ideal mother, the gypsy-mother, usurped control of his consciousness. He reintegrated her power, but did not yet begin the difficult process of redifferentiation. He behaved like a caveman, until the discrepancy between his conduct and the requirements of our civilization stalled him completely.

Even then, regression continued. The earliest, most primitive images lost their specific forms; the "unconscious of the past" was gone; the debts of history were cancelled; the crisis reached its apex; the door to the real center was unlocked; and the future with its unknown values and formative forces drew him in a new direction. The "unconscious of the future" began like the dawn of morning to filter into his consciousness. And his first discovery in this new way of life was the experience that objective consciousness is We-consciousness, that our most genuine interest is the welfare of our fellow-men rather than our individual welfare. When he went down and hit the rock bottom of life he found love.

3. The New Life

The crisis, as we see, is the point where we are forsaken by the "unconscious of the past." The chains of cause and effect, all the things which are determined and may determine us, are of no avail. Not even our oldest images, representing all the inheritance of the race, can show us the way out. In such a trial we need something more, beyond the stored-up wisdom of the race, beyond the past, beyond time and space. We need creation, or we perish.

The intensity and depth of our crises vary from a few moments of utmost despair to several months of complete melancholy or a vague sense of depression which may last many years. A good many steps of the way can evidently be worked out in the unconscious, and sometimes the mature results enter our consciousness after some weeks of preparation; yet we may have been unaware of this preparation except perhaps for an incomprehensible sleepiness, tiredness or general restlessness.

The more we can observe the details of the process the more we discover the well known features of the "Great Turn," or the "Great Way," as it has been described by spiritual leaders all through the history of religion. Seen from the viewpoint of depth-psychology the essential stages of the journey are three.

The first stage is regression and reintegration. It corresponds to the "purgation" of medieval mysticism. The Ego or the idol, the rigid structure of the former life, collapses, together with all its valuations, prejudices, resentments, desires and fears. The "censorship," the screen between consciousness and the unconscious, breaks down. Old images, forgotten emotions, repressed functions, come to life again; primitive obsessions and projections, visions and nightmares endanger the equilibrium of the good citizen. Without adequate inner or outer help, religious and psychological, he will be in an evil predicament.

This is the situation which the psalmists have described with amazing exactitude: "The sorrows of death compassed me, and the floods of ungodly men made me afraid. The sorrows of hell compassed me about: the snares of death prevented me" (Psalm 18:4, 5). And again: "Many bulls have compassed me: strong bulls of Bashan have beset me round" (Psalm 22:12). The outer and the inner evil fuse; death or insanity seem to be certain; all the negativity of the universe seems to be arrayed against us. There is only one way out: the religious way: "Yea, though I walk through the valley of the shadow of death, I will fear no evil: for thou art with me" (Psalm 23:4).

The power of the images, terrifying as it may be, is borrowed power. It appears to be genuine and invincible only as long as we do not know the real center. The appeal to the center, therefore, is the only thing left for the person who is "beset by the bulls" of the collective unconscious. Even the atheist, if anything disagreeable takes him by surprise, reacts with a superficial turn to the center. He says "O God!" or "For goodness sake!" If the believer can do the same thing in a more serious way, even though in the moment of fear or pain his concept of God may be vague or childish, it will help him more than anything else.

The turning towards the center is the second stage of the journey. But the center itself, the aspect of God which can be experienced in such a situation, is quite different from what most people expect it to be. Either we project some learned or emotional ideas into the universe; or, knowing we must have no image of God, we use an empty frame, three feet square, and according to our creed we think God will fit the frame. Yet, he does not. His appearance, if he appears at all, crushes our beautiful frame. We are frightened and offended and decree that the power which destroyed our convictions must be the devil.

The nearer we come to the center, the more we leave the images behind, the more are our fears turned into anxiety. And anxiety, if we face it, is turned into awe. What seemed to be the power of darkness now manifests itself as the power of light. After the great and strong wind comes the earthquake, then the fire, and then the still small voice (I Kings 19:11–13).

The terrible and destructive aspect of the godhead—the "tremendum" in theological language—originates as a subjective human experience, though an unavoidable one if our religious convictions and our rigid theology are smashed by the Grace of God. We live in a jail which we call our castle; a foreign soldier breaks through the doors, come to free us by blasting the walls of our castle—and we fight him with the last might of our broken Ego, calling him scoundrel, knave and devil, until we are exhausted, overwhelmed and disarmed. Then looking at the victor with disinterested objectivity we recognize him: St. Michael smilingly sheathes his sword.

The power which brought about the fight was grace. The "evil" which caused our anxiety was, in the last analysis, grace. And even the real scoundrels, our competitors in egocentricity who betrayed us and wounded us so unjustly, even they, as we discover now, were already working unknowingly and unwillingly in the service of the super-human strategy of grace. This fact is no excuse for their evil-doing; but it shows the transcendent power and wisdom of the coming Kingdom of Heaven. And above all it shows that the Kingdom is there already and is working in spite of and even through the errors and felonies of its prospective citizens.

Here begins the third stage of the journey, identical with the "illumination" of the old mystics. It is not only an intellectual insight but is at the same time an emotional experience of utmost reality and a volitional change which overthrows the whole system of our values, goals and means. It gives us a new viewpoint, or rather a double viewpoint, which enables us to see people at the same time as rascals and as children of God. Evil reveals its creative implications, and what we deemed to be good now shows its fiendish danger as the devil's bait. Deeper insight, more power, increasing responsibility, and above all a higher kind of love, more detached and more comprehensive— these are the characteristics of the new life, as far as we are able to describe them in the language of our empirical, and that means humanly limited, psychology.

The "unconscious of the past," we may say, was conditioned by our images and their historical forms. The "unconscious of the future" is conditioned only by the center itself. It is creative power, using the images, now cleansed and timeless, according to its creative plans, which are our own unconscious goals. The crisis then is the transition from an eccentric, less conscious and less powerful life—pivoting around the Ego-image or an idolized image —to a well-centered, more conscious and more powerful life—pivoting around the real Self. This Self proves to be the center both of the individual and of the group, and therefore transforms the individual into a servant of the group—that is love; and proves to be also our relation to God, and therefore transforms individuals and groups into servants of God—that is faith. The crisis, if it is complete, means conversion.*

Our concept of "crisis" coincides with the meaning of the Greek word METANOIA (Matt. 3:2, 8; Mark 1:4), which is rather inadequately translated as "repentance." The imperative "repent!" should not be interpreted, as some modern commentators do, as "change your mind!" No one can change his mind purposefully except for the replacement of one eccentric view by another equally eccentric view. No one can voluntarily decrease his egocentricity or idolatry. The only thing we can do, and the only useful interpretation of the central Christian imperative is: do not run away from your crises; try to stand the impact of reality and to discover the light behind darkness; do not resist evil. Then evil will be found to be grace.

We have seen and can see every day how people are forced into their crises by the consequences of their deviations, and how skillfully they try to escape. Some are caught and ground in the mills of grace, which appear to be cruel and almost sadistic if looked upon from the viewpoint of Egos and idols. Some escape time and again, postponing their crises and increasing the sum total of their debts. And some seem to need not an earthly crisis but a metaphysical one: they have to go through "the eonian

* What the mystics called "union" is a later event.

fire," the fire between the eons or world-ages. (The translation "everlasting fire" is incorrect; something which is beyond time cannot last). And some, as Jesus said, "will never see death" if they obey his teaching (John 8:51, Moffatt).

There is evidently a way which leads us through the crisis without the great tribulation or the eonian fire. And Christianity is certainly the way, or at least a way, of achieving this. If our psychology is truly religious it must enable us to do what humanly can be done to find this better way, and to become a servant of God, cooperating with His will in His creation. Such religious Self-Education will therefore be the test stone of our psychology.

Part Three

DEPTH-PSYCHOLOGY IN
SELF-EDUCATION

INTRODUCTORY NOTE

This is the third time that the author has tried to discuss the problems of self-education as seen from the viewpoint of depth-psychology. His first attempt was made in *God Helps Those* (written 1929, English edition 1931); the second in *How Character Develops* (together with Roy Dickerson in 1939). The relationship of the three books is such that the later one always includes, deepens and enlarges the insight of the earlier ones.

In 1929 it was not yet possible to explain the whole process on the basis of a simple dynamic concept of human life, as has been attempted in the following chapters. The valuable contribution in *God Helps Those* consisted in the case histories. They contain and illustrate the principles which were not yet recognizable. *How Character Develops* was intended as a primer. It gives simple rules and ideas which have proved rather useful in the early stages of self-education.

The present book is the first attempt to present the whole problem systematically. It discusses the essential viewpoints and therefore seeks to be comprehensive, precise and terse. Wherever the reader misses the practical application he should go back to *How Character Develops.* There he will find the "How"; here he will see the "Why." Most people, however, if they really understand the "Why," should be able to discover the "How" by themselves. That is better than reading it in a book.

One important subject has not yet been described in this connection: the analysis of our own dreams. In spite of its importance this material is omitted. A short discussion, such as would have been possible within the scope of our book, would seem to be useless. These difficult problems require a whole book in themselves.*

* In the meantime the reader must be referred to the writings of C. G. Jung and Frances Wickes, as listed in the bibliography at the end of the book.

PROBLEMS

The human predicament is obvious. We misunderstand, misuse and repress the creative powers which are entrusted to us. They turn into the negative and destroy us, unless we find a way out. This has been seen more or less clearly for at least three thousand years. Accordingly innumerable remedies have been recommended and tried. But the result has been deplorable: except for a few great leaders, a few individual saints, and some small groups which experimented with a new kind of community, the rest is mediocrity—merely conscious good will based on a foundation of unconscious negativity.

If we try to help others, forgetting our own worries, we are told: "Why do you note the splinter in your brother's eye and fail to see the plank in your own eye?" (Matt. 7:3, Moffatt). And if we try to work out our own salvation we discover that we are interested only in our private welfare and in the immortality of our dear Ego. What is the way out?

The way out is clearly described in the words of the New Testament: "Your light is to shine before men, that they may see the good you do and glorify your Father in Heaven" (Matt. 5:16, Moffatt). Our positive power, if only we could develop it, would help others without our "taking splinters out of their eyes." Thus we have to go back, after all, to the plank in our own eye. How can we remove it? What are the ways and means of religious self-education?

Let us keep in mind that the endeavor of self-education will be thwarted by the egocentricity of its motives, unless the process of development brings about a thorough revision of its own motivation. We should try, therefore, from the beginning, to eliminate egocentric motives as much as possible. Especially dangerous is the egocentric admixture in our social, moral and religious goals. "I want to go this way, and I am ready to pay the highest price for the training, because I want to be a better social worker, psychologist, teacher or preacher, in order to lead others on the right way." This motive is wrong unless it is completed by the thought: "and I would go this way even if I should have to give up all preaching, teaching, consulting and social work."

Even immaculate goals such as scientific research, or the simple conviction that it is our moral duty to improve our characters, cannot provide an adequate motive. A high-ranking scholar of theology has tried hard to go through the experiences of depth-psychology, in order to investigate its values for Christian life in general and for his denomination in particular. His unconscious remained completely blocked, giving him not one single dream. Now he is convinced that there is no such thing as depth in psychology at all, and that the whole related literature is "mere fantasy." In these cases the goal is impersonal; some idea, cause or value is at stake, and the person is only a means in the service of this goal. Experience, however, has shown that religious self-education bears fruit only if the motive is exclusively personal. The motive must be personal, though not egocentric. The mature, unegoistic personality should be the goal.

God wants the person rather than the cause. He creates men, not books, or organizations; actions rather than ideas are His concern. That seems to be the unanimous teaching not only of Jesus and the Jewish prophets, but also of Buddha and Lao-Tse.

The ideal motive, then, would be God's own command, the voice which told Jonah to go to Nineveh and Jesus to go to the desert in order to be tempted. But we are rather deaf, nowadays, or we mistake the stirring of some unconscious egocentric desire for the voice of the Lord. We should make provision, therefore, for a huge dose of skepticism with regard to all the impulses which arise during our silent worship and meditation and prayer. The devil, especially in his rôle of the lawyer of our Egos, imitates perfectly the appearance of an angel, using for his own purposes the power of our unconscious imagery, which we frequently mistake for the power of the Lord.

Fortunately God uses many languages. If we do not listen to the "still small voice" he may express himself more urgently in storms and floods, and if we misunderstand him again he may try to help us by unleashing the earthquake. The language which we understand best is suffering. That is why the mourners are blessed; and that is why suffering, either our own or our friends' suffering of which we may be a cause, is the best and most efficient goad towards self-education.

But the aim should not be just removal of suffering, or as the physicians' aim is, restoration of health as it used to be. Suffering should make us aware of the fact that there is a higher goal, and that more suffering is in store if we fail to reach this goal. The dynamics of our situation which provide the motive, the power, and the direction of the whole process is this: we have to grow, to develop our mature personalities, or we shall perish.

The goal may now be defined as expanding consciousness (Gerald Heard); integration of the personality (C. G. Jung); the growing We-experience, as we would call it; or membership in the mystical body of Christ, as St. Paul has described it. The decisive point is that the goal of our self-education must not be an arbitrary idea about what we want to be like. It has to be the very goal of human history, the will of God; and its ways and means have to be the ways and means of human development. We can only bring about what reality would produce anyhow: but it is possible to do it with less waste of time and effort, avoiding detours, errors and, above all, our usual egocentric escapes.

This presupposes, of course, a method of finding out what may be the desirable step, the creative reaction, in every given situation. The general direction of development—expanding consciousness, the integrated personality, the We-experience—is known, as is the general religious command "Love your neighbor." The question remains however, what we can do to develop all this, if so far we only feel distrust and competition? Here depth-psychology can make a decisive contribution which, together with the traditional experience of Christianity, may be able to solve this problem for a large number of believers and seekers.

Such cooperation with life, or to put it religiously, with creation, looks rather satisfactory at first sight. Soon however we come to face three serious obstacles.

The first is a moralistic one. By analyzing ourselves, it is said, we shall grow even more egocentric. Introspection leads us into all kinds of vanity, until finally our main occupation will consist in writing a diary, and our chief interest will lie in becoming a more exceptional case. Answer: This is true, if the original motive was too egocentric. But if sleeplessness or marital troubles gave the incentive, be sure your pains and sorrows will prevent your becoming an interesting case. Therefore it would be better to wait until the situation is disagreeable enough.

The second objection is a religious one. Self-education, it says, is self-salvation. We cannot work out our own salvation. We are saved "by grace alone"; therefore we should wait until the grace of God makes us see that we have already been saved two thousand years ago. If you believe in the blood of the lamb no self-education is needed, and if you do not believe, no self-education can help you. Answer: It is true, many of the imperatives of the New Testament, especially such as the one in the letters of Paul "let us cleanse ourselves" (II Cor. 7:1), are addressed to people who have already received the Holy Spirit. Therefore they apply, nowadays, to almost no one. But there are other imperatives and admonitions for beginners and seekers who are not yet saved: "ask . . . seek . . . knock!" (Matt. 7:7); "make terms with your opponent!" (Matt. 5:25, Moffatt); then, time and again: "forgive!" (Mat. 6:14, 15); and above all the very essence of Christian self-education—or as we may say more exactly, of self-education towards Christianity: METANO-EITE! And remember, it means not only "repent!" (Matt. 3:2). It means "go through your crises, whether it takes you one year or ten!"

All these imperatives, summed up in the paradoxical command "love your enemy," imply self-education. And they need careful psychological explanation and application. Otherwise our "education" will take place without our knowledge, against our will, and in the negative direction. The result will be what we see everywhere in so-called Christian communities: repression, unconscious vices, hatred and envy in the disguise of love, and cowardice hidden behind big empty words.

The third and most serious objection is a psychological one. Our purpose includes, among other difficult things, the integration of our conscious personality. That means the acceptance and assimilation of unconscious contents, such as repressed desires and undeveloped capacities, into our conscious mind. How can we do this? Our Ego does not want to see the things which would destroy it. Its resistance against the conquest of the unconscious is a struggle for survival. Only an objective helper, a psychologist, a modern father-confessor, can overcome this resistance.

Answer: This would be true if there were only one evil,

one Shadow, one darkness. But evil is always manifold; and its different forms are contradictory and antagonistic. In time the Shadow, for instance irritability, will increase to the point where you identify yourself with its tendencies: "I am furious!" and then you will disown and condemn your former Ego, the softness and smugness of the pseudo-Christian. The Ego and its Shadow are equally evil; blaming each other they bring to light hidden hideousness. All our unconscious deviations and possibilities will become conscious if we go on raging against ourselves —which is the very meaning of the word "crisis." All we need, in addition to suffering, courage and patience, is a good, simple and clear psychology of the unconscious; a zoology, as it were, which teaches us how to deal with the beasts of our unconscious Zoo. Then our courage will grow into faith, and finally we will be able to face the lions in Daniel's den. Your unconscious resistance is the stronger the less faith you have; and vice versa.

The discoveries of depth-psychology enable us to revitalize most of the treasures hidden in Christian and other religious traditions. Meditation and prayer, art, music, dancing and dramatics, auto-suggestion, and even fasting and the practice of alms appear in a thoroughly new light. The arsenal of Christian tools, which had been reduced to mere intellectualism by the iconoclasts of the last four centuries, will be restored in an entirely new sense (which means a very old sense). The Saints reappear from the limbo of the unconscious; but now they are not heavenly officials beyond space and time, they are inner realities, collective images and powers which have to be cultivated, revered and used. And they must be carefully distinguished from the real center; they must not become idols.

No one should be lured without urgent necessity to enter this turmoil of creativity and spirituality. If you are allowed to stay where you are, you had better stay. No curiosity, no scientific purpose, no moral duty gives you the right or even the possibility of going through the purgatory of depth-psychology. The only ticket of admission is personal suffering. And the reason, one of the reasons, is this: dozens of collective and personal convictions, opinions and prejudices have to be burned or melted away; much criticism, indignation and fear, a host of emotional restrictions veiled in intellectual "knowledge," have to disappear before the doors of depth-psychology open up. And since religious self-education, at least this special way of religious self-education, is based on depth-psychology, the conditions of failure and success are both religious and psychological.

For whom then is this way possible? What are the minimum requirements for those who want to make this attempt? From the religious side two things are needed. First, the belief, or at least the suspicion, that there is or may be—as William James puts it—"an unseen order, and that our supreme good lies in harmoniously adjusting ourselves thereto." * And, secondly, a certain tolerance towards God, which means our readiness to allow God to be as he wants to be and not as we expect him to be according to our own conceptions, theologies and creeds (and our interpretation of the Bible which we think is the only right

* *The Varieties of Religious Experience,* Lecture II.

interpretation). We should give Him the chance to teach us something new about Himself. On the psychological side we need a certain amount of personal suffering, as we have pointed out; and a certain readiness to admit that something may be wrong in our own inner structure. If these four requirements have not yet been met we should wait. There is no hurry, for the inner situation will be better prepared when we begin some years later. And it is never too late.

II

PRINCIPLES

From the foregoing considerations we can easily derive the main principles which should govern our religious self-education. Three of them apply to self-education because they are general principles of human life, and self-education is part of our human life, focalized and concentrated; the other three furnish the practical basis of our endeavor.

1. *Creativity*.

The first principle has been mentioned already: it is the simple fact that we can and should achieve only what the tendency of evolution (if you prefer the secular expression) or the will of God (if you choose the religious term) want us to do and will finally force us to do. This principle, of course, includes the decisive presupposition that there is a will of God and that God is creative; or that there is a tendency of evolution; and that both the will of God and the tendency of evolution can either be obeyed or disregarded. If you do not believe this, or if, at a minimum, you cannot assume this at least as a working hypothesis, you cannot undertake religious self-education, and must try to live without it as long as you can.

2. *Freedom.*

The second principle concerns the relation between the human being and the aims of his development (whether they are termed evolution or the will of God). We are not only free to neglect these aims purposefully for a long time, committing conscious sins; we are free also, and indeed much more inclined, to miss them by mistake, forgetting, confusing, misinterpreting them. Thus we commit unconscious sins and produce biological deviations (for example, through the wrong diet, alcohol, wrong marriage, wrong vocation, etc.) as well as philosophical errors (for example, wrong theologies, morals, laws, etc.) and psychological blunders (for example, repression of useful capacities or transmutation of virtues into vices).

Being subject to deviations, we cannot know for sure what our next step has to be. Neither science nor theology nor ethics can teach us what is right or wrong in a given situation. Otherwise there would be no decision, responsibility or creativity on our part. If you think all "commandments" are written in the Bible, just watch your child: he desperately wants, let us say, more ice cream. If you give it to him you will spoil him, and he will hate you later when he finds out. If you do not give it to him, you will disappoint him, and he will hate you now and later too. The will of God requires us, as far as we can see, to be creative. He has created the world; could not you, His child, at least create a satisfactory solution of the ice cream problem? You cannot find it in books: you must be creative yourself. And you cannot be sure about the result: you must take the risk. You may be wrong; you may do harm to your child; both you and he will bear the consequences. The principle is: be creative, at the risk of failure; and if you fail, do not give up; be creative again.

3. *Faith.*

Our freedom to choose the right or the wrong way should fill us with enthusiasm because it enables us to be creative, to find the new way, the unheard of solution. On the other hand it should make us humble because it means that many of our decisions may be wrong. The third principle, therefore, is that all our decisions, judgments and convictions should be temporary, open to criticism and adjustable to further development. In particular, "Do not judge," do not condemn anybody; you can be certain that you do not know him thoroughly.

On the other hand we have to act. We must give ourselves entirely to a cause, a vocation, a love, for instance, when choosing a wife or husband, a profession, a creed. Those decisions should be final. The ensuing actions cannot be undone; and yet they have to be based on judgments which are admittedly imperfect, immature and subject to further development. How can we put at stake our lives and what is more, the lives of our friends and relatives, in the service of a goal which ten years from now may appear in a quite different light? The answer is: faith.

We cannot act and therefore we cannot live unless we believe that life is creative and that even our errors—though they may engender infinite suffering—will finally be stepping stones of evolution. Evolution, consequently, has to be understood as transcending space and time. It has to be the religious, not the biological concept of evolution.

If you kill yourself and some friends in an automobile accident the damage may be enormous. The redemption may presuppose other worlds and future lives; at least the compensation cannot be found on our earth—and still there will be redemption. If you do not believe this, you have to renounce religious self-education as it is discussed here. So you had better ask and seek and knock in order to find that faith, that confidence in the creative will of God (which now turns out to be the basis of evolution) who will help us to pay all our debts or to cancel them instantly if we dare to trust His grace.

For the purposes of religious self-education the three principles, creativity, freedom and faith should be combined in the following way: We should learn to cooperate with the creative will of God, which means we should develop our own creativity. God has created us as creative beings and therefore given us freedom to err; we have erred for thousands of years, we are deeply deviated, we shall err again; but we must take the risk, bear the consequences, pay the price; otherwise we can never find the way out. And we can take the terrible responsibility for our future errors only if we can find, gradually or suddenly, the trust in God's creativity which time and again restores us as His children.

The practical steps which can and should be made in this direction will be discussed in the following chapter. These steps are psychological because they influence the structure of our character, changing vices into virtues and replacing inhibitions by capacities; and they are religious because their final goal is faith, receptivity to grace, and the very entrance into the Kingdom of Heaven.

Grace given from above and faith found within oneself are identical for the one who has them; yet they seem to be separate entities as long as we cannot reach them. Many people feel: I am unworthy of grace because I have no faith; and I have no faith as long as grace is missing. The solution of this seemingly insoluble problem, and therefore the all-powerful center of religious life and religious self-education, can be easily recognized by those who have experienced its might: it is the Spirit. If we need a more exact expression, to distinguish this Spirit from its egocentric caricature, human intellect, we may call it with St. Paul: "the Spirit of God" which makes us "sons of God" (Rom. 8:14, Moffatt) or "the Spirit of Christ" (Rom. 8:9, Moffatt); they are one and the same. We may call it the eternal spirit which appears to us as "the unconscious of the future." It is the principle of principles in human life.

However, many people, serious seekers after faith and truth, tell you honestly that they have never seen a really religious person and especially never a Christian. They have always been disappointed, betrayed and cheated by wolves in sheep's clothing, false prophets, idolaters and hypocrites. Moreover, they know history; they remember the thousands of heretics and witches burnt in the name of Christ. And they know that no dogma or creed or interpretation of texts stands uncontradicted. Therefore the word "Christ" makes them suspicious; they shrug their shoulders and turn away.

If a genuine Christian has to deal with these victims of pseudo-religion he should not preach or discuss, but live Christianity. Only his creative life can undo the results of irreligious and therefore destructive lives. And if the reader of this book happens to be himself such a victim of false prophets he should not worry about names. He should ask and knock and seek; when the door opens he will know where he is. He has not even to believe firmly in the three principles of creativity, freedom and faith. It is enough, at the beginning, if he can accept them as working hypotheses.

4. *Polarity.*

The other three principles refer to our practical work. Its basis is the principle of polarity. "Differentiation" unfolds life in innumerable pairs of opposites, such as young and old, masculine and feminine, expansion and contraction, tension and relaxation, etc. "Integration" keeps them in balance and enables the creative center to use them alternatively without preference. "Disintegration" disturbs the balance: one extreme is favored and developed, the opposite is repressed, stunted and turned into the negative; and the center is superseded by a pseudo-center, namely the Ego or an idol.

Self-education, therefore, and all psycho-therapy, tries to reestablish the sovereignty of the center by reintegrating the pairs of opposites. Our way is the discovery of hidden talents and the rehabilitation of possibilities which have been in disgrace for many years. We are looking for the virtues within or behind the vices. Our goal is the redemption of that which was lost. If education is the straightforward development of interests and capacities which are consciously acknowledged, our work should be called reeducation. We constitute a rescue squad rather than guides. Our endeavor is a search for unknown treasures, a mining in the depth of the unconscious. We want to change the negative into positive power, and destruction into creation. And therefore we have to learn how to face, and if necessary to provoke and to unmask, the powers of Hell.

5. *Tolerance.*

The next principle follows logically: Tolerance. We must not fight against the negative powers which we hope to transform into positive values. This refers to outer as well as inner evils. Distrust, competition, calumny, betrayal, persecution, hatred—arising against us in the outer world—provide good opportunities for self-education. Distrust, aversion, disgust, fear, greed, passion, compulsion, anxiety—arising within our own mind—are even better. They force us to deal with the negative powers and to discover their true location within ourselves.

The great imperative "Do not resist evil" should not be misunderstood as ethical advice. A moralist who says "you must not resist evil" could just as well say that water ought to run uphill. Not resisting evil is an art which requires practice, wisdom, discipline and above all, faith. It does not mean, of course, to submit to evil, to yield or to connive at it. It means acceptance without cooperation;

tolerance, sympathy, and confidence in the final positive outcome. To learn this art of not resisting evil is already a decisive part of our self-education.

The first application of the principle of tolerance may be described in some detail because of its practical importance. It is tolerance towards our own inner life, or psychological honesty. In watching our emotional reactions, remembrances, blunders, "distractions" and dreams we may discover, and indeed we want to discover, our own hidden vices, our unconscious and repressed ugliness, in the hope that finally it may turn into beauty. These discoveries are painful and sometimes unbearable. Sometimes we may be frightened by our own passions, revengefulness or hatred; at other times we may be ashamed of the complete emptiness and dryness of our inner life; or we may be convinced that we will lose our minds.

Not to resist our inner evil, to be tolerant towards our own wickedness, wretchedness, or stupidity is more difficult than to be the martyr of outer enemies. Fortunately we are not alone on this frightful road. The writer of the Twenty-third Psalm has gone through the same experience. And the great religious self-educator, Saint Paul, has left us the compass of his inner journey: "I am certain neither death nor life, neither angels nor principalities, neither the present nor the future, no powers of the Height or of the Depth, nor anything else in all creation will be able to part us from God's love in Christ Jesus our Lord" (Rom. 8:38, 39, Moffatt).

The cowardice of later centuries, however, has found a new escape for Egos and Idols: the wrong use of a valuable tool, namely of meditation. "Concentrate on good thoughts. Meditate on the words 'God is love.' Do not permit any distraction. Do not indulge in personal sorrows. And especially, do not hate or condemn or despise any one or anything." This mental discipline is good if it is balanced by the opposite discipline, namely the discipline of reckless honesty: tell yourself and tell God what you are really like. If wisely guided the meditator can solve a large part of his problems by meditating on negative symbols. If this "negative" part of his practice is omitted he is in danger of producing an additional repression. He deprives himself of his creative forces, shuts them up in the unconscious and becomes paler, softer and weaker every day.

Our way is this: pour out all your fears and anxieties, malicious joy and greed and hatred, and you will be astonished at the terrific amount of power which is pent up in your unconscious mind. We can release this power and transform it from negative into positive power, only by bringing it into the open, into the light of consciousness, and by accepting ourselves as we are, even though the mountain of debts seems to crush us. This is the principle of honesty. And it is clear that it can be applied only if connected with the principle of faith which we described above. The two together constitute the next principle: forgiveness.

6. *Forgiveness.*

The principle of forgiveness in its psychological application embodies the same mutuality as in its original formulation (Matt. 6:14, 15, Moffatt). "If you forgive

men their trespasses, then your heavenly Father will forgive you; but if you do not forgive men, your Father will
not forgive your trespasses either." But we have to add an
important fact which in the New Testament is little
stressed though not missing: the dead men's bones within
the whitewashed tombs—the fact that many evils persist in
our unconscious unforgiven; and they cannot be forgiven
as long as they are repressed.

We harbor unconscious hatred of forgotten origin, perhaps an early betrayal by mother or aunt. We may discover that unconscious anxiety absorbs all our creative
power, because we felt, when two years old, that our father
did not love us enough. To bring to light the buried skeletons of our early tragedies, to understand that the evil-
doers who almost killed us were the victims of other
evil-doers, and that those again did not know how to love,
because they were betrayed by their own parents:—that
means to acknowledge the wickedness of mankind and to
forgive full-heartedly because we ourselves are badly in
need of forgiveness for the ugly things which we have
done.

Even before we feel that we are forgiven, and that the
whole debt is cancelled, we may realize the amazing
change from darkness to light and from hatred to love.
We may have hated the one who spanked us or spoiled
us and thus made our lives miserable for thirty or forty
years. In the next moment we may see as clearly as in a
dramatic vision this person, forty years earlier, being himself spanked or spoiled by some one else who was supposed
to love him dearly. There is only one possibility left: love

and compassion and the ardent impulse to help mankind to get rid of this tragedy. And we join the army of love.

The same power which was hatred, revengefulness, resentfulness or bitterness, now flows through us as love, courage and initiative. Suddenly we know what we have to do. The negative image, the channel of negative power, is now changed into a positive symbol, charged with the creative might of the real center. Forgiveness, if it is genuine, immediately releases the creative and spiritual power which we have called the unconscious of the future. If this sign is missing we may be certain that we have not yet been forgiven because we ourselves have not yet forgiven.

III

METHODS

How can we find our real center? How can we get rid of the Ego or of the Idol? The first answer that arises in individual life as well as in the life of the race is the imperative: "Thou shalt not . . ." Not to steal, not to tell lies, and so on—these "negative" commandments are necessary wherever individuals have to grope their way from the original tribal consciousness to the mature universal consciousness. They are much-needed implements of social security until we grow mature enough to realize our individual responsibility for all human life. Then we will no longer need general, prohibitive commandments; and the positive creative orders, the Will of God, will be understood and obeyed immediately.

The "Law"—its morality, and especially its application in bringing up children—is a temporary though unavoidable stop-gap which is easily misused and which then produces the opposite of the expected result. If we were saints we could tell our children "you must not . . ." without poisoning them. Yet in such a case they would need no law, not being thrown into egocentricity by egocentric parents. As it is, we are not saints, and we unknowingly misuse the commands (which are God's) in the service of our own purposes (which are egocentric). We say: "You must not disturb your father's nap," as if it were God's nap, because we are not creative enough to give the children a creative occupation which would make them grow and would keep them quite naturally from disturbing their father's rest.

Moral commandments usually arouse egocentricity, either egocentric resistance or egocentric obedience (the "good child" and the "bad child" being equally egocentric), because even the best moral laws are enforced by egocentric authorities, and unconscious egocentric implications cannot be avoided even in their most careful applications. This is our psychological contribution to St. Paul's philosophy of the Law (Rom. 7).

Later, when the victims of our misused morality reach the age of self-responsibility and self-education, the only viewpoint they are able to apply to their inner lives is the moralistic command. Yet now the negative imperative "I must not . . . ," the cause of repression, is completed by the positive imperative "I must . . ." which tries to overcome the result of repression without however repealing repression itself. For twenty years a man may have thought sexuality evil; then, in order to be a good husband, he wants to be potent, affectionate, passionate, although sexuality in general still remains an evil to him. He kills his horse and then blames it for not pulling the wagon. We make this mistake not only in the field of sexual life but also in the fields of courage, initiative, self-confidence, emotional honesty, and so on.

The pale-blooded, nervous person, sickly and irritable,

suffers from repressed—that is, unlived—life. The moralistic method, which is always the conservative method, cannot help him at all. Thus history makes its counterthrust with the liberal idea of "letting go." Relax! do not worry about what people will say! show yourself as you are! be confident! trust your instinct! nature is good! you are all right if you are free! In ethics, theology, mysticism ("New Thought"), psychology (Sigmund Freud), education (Alfred Adler) and social life we find the unanimous conviction that everything would be fine if only we could replace repression by its opposite: honest and unrestricted expression.

In some cases, to a certain extent, this "expressionism" is a useful method of self-education; and in education it is at least better than repression. If you have to write a letter it is better to wait until a creative mood moves you to write. If you force yourself, without the creative urge, your letter will be poor and shallow. In many cases, however, your creativity may never move you; or what you think to be creativity may turn out to be a superficial egocentric illusion.

On the whole, the method of unrestricted self-expression has not borne the fruit which its prophets expected. There is not less unlived life nowadays than there was one hundred years ago: it is only that other functions are repressed. Our liberal life now allows all kinds of sexual satisfactions—but real love is almost forbidden. Loyalty is deemed to be stupid, promiscuity is "natural"; one hundred years ago the opposite was the case. From the psychological viewpoint both valuations are equally wrong, and the corresponding methods of education and self-education, namely repression and expression, have equally failed. Repression can neither be avoided nor undone by expression.

The trouble is that even under the most liberal system of life we do not dare to express what we really are. Repression is the result of early fear; and it began long before any educational principles became efficient. Its cause is not lack of pedagogical insight but lack of creativity, which indicates lack of faith on the part of the adults. The child was afraid, for instance, to show his childish heart to the older brother who ridiculed him so successfully. And the parents did not know how to help him. So he decided, unconsciously, that love and loyalty were not permissible. And he learned to repress his tender emotions and to express the opposite: scorn and malice. Thirty years later he tries to express freely all that he can find within himself. What does he find? No great love, no passion, nothing of all the things which he wants to develop. But if he is honest enough, not resisting his inner evil, he may discover a vague tendency to torture his brother who had tortured him. If he would dare now to express himself recklessly— would he go and kill his brother? Perhaps. Or he may write a furious letter, hateful, silly, and completely out of place.

Thus, we see that it is certainly better not to act upon all the tendencies and urges which we may discover in the deeper layers of our unconscious mind. Revengefulness, hatred, envy, greed and anxiety would upset our family life and our social position. If all repressions were released at once in a big city, the city would be an insane asylum with insane wardens. It happens partially during riots and revolutions; and to a slighter degree it is officially permitted (and controlled) as a kind of safety valve, in the carnivals of the southern countries, the countries with less rigid repression.

If you repress what you harbor, you will be stifled by your own unlived life. If you express the repressed tendencies, you may destroy and kill. You must find another way to "make terms with your opponent, so long as you and he are on the way to court" (Matt. 5:25, Moffatt). The way out, indeed the only way out, as far as we know, is the way of confession. But the word confession must be understood, and the method must be used in the right way, according to the structure of the human mind and the special problems of our time. Otherwise the result will be the opposite of what it should be.

Originally there were two people involved, the confessing initiate and the priest, the father confessor; or, since the ministry has lost the knowledge and the power of the confessional way, the psychologist. But the latter is often as poorly equipped for this dangerous work as is the minister.

Imagine the confessional process in all its crudity and ruthlessness. It is a powerful and dangerous discharge of high voltage; and if you are not an expert in this field you had better stay away—or defend yourself by assuming the rôle of a judge. If you judge, you turn confession into new repression. Where there is judgment, there is no truth. And absolution is judgment, too. If some one confesses in order to be absolved he is unable to confess the "hidden sins," namely the darkness of his unconscious mind.

The superficial deeds which he remembers can be easily told and are easily plucked, but these are only the poisonous flowers blossoming above the earth. The roots remain in the unconscious, and they will thrive again and again—new flowers, new sins to be confessed daily. And both the sinner and the absolver live in an unconscious agreement never to touch the poisonous roots, because the same explosion, the same revolution would upset the whole outer and inner lives of father confessor and parishioner alike. "Keep off!! High Voltage!!" That is one of the reasons why two thousand years of confessional practice have failed to discover the unconscious. The result of this wrong practice is that scarcely anything can be more boring and more useless psychologically than the usual routine of confession.

We have to revitalize, indeed to recreate, the meaning of the old and colorful word, if we can use it at all. And we try to do so by stressing two aspects of its meaning: one being known, but too much neglected so far, the other being quite new and, as far as we can see, included only vaguely in some old descriptions.

The first aspect is that the nearer mankind draws to real Christianity the more the Christian can and should confess to the One who was always supposed to be represented by, or present in, the Father Confessor, namely God. A trustworthy friend, a father confessor, if possible an expert in depth-psychology, should be available in case of emergency. But the main part of the task has to be solved by the individual alone by himself in confessional meditation; and that means "in the presence of God." Try to pour out before Him whatever comes to your mind. Be not embarrassed by His presence. Do not refrain from strong words —say "swine" if you mean swine; God knows what you say and what you do not say anyhow. He knows your conscious and your unconscious mind equally. Therefore His presence will help you to discover your "secret sins" and unearth your "buried talents."

Here we reach the second point: our confession has to bring to light the unknown, the unconscious darkness, and the undeveloped creativity of our deeper layers. Confession then becomes research, investigation, discovery. We discover our individual as well as collective drives, too much and too little power, emotional drought and emotional floods, destructive and constructive urges, our animal nature and our vegetal nature. If we can spread out before Him all the hidden roots of our virtues and vices, if we are honest and courageous enough to release before Him the high voltage of our unconscious hatred and love, we may discover that all our power is in the last analysis His power, and that our darkness turns into light because He is both darkness and light.

Expression of what we find within ourselves, honest and reckless expression before the face of the Eternal, assuming responsibility for what we are, even if we are unaware of it, and asking God to help us to master the wild horses, or to revive the skeletons of horses which we dig out during the long hours of our confessions—this is the psychological method of religious self-education. It is a way of bringing to consciousness our unconscious contents, and of establishing control over our hidden powers. It is the way to mature responsibility. It is the old way of the Psalmist: "Yet who can detect his lapses? Absolve me from my faults unknown! And hold thy servant back from wilful sins, from giving way to them" (Psalm 19:12, 13, Moffatt).

Not in the presence of a minister or a psychologist, but in the presence of God, things change completely. If you hate your brother, and you pour out all your hatred, remembering at the same time, as much as you can, the presence of God—and your hatred does not change, then you are not sufficiently aware either of the presence of God or of your hatred, and probably of neither. Be more honest, give vent to your emotions. You hate your brother: imagine his presence, before God tell him how you feel, kick him, scratch him. You are ten years old now—get up from your chair, don't pretend to be a wise old Buddha, pace the floor, yell, scream, punch the furniture, express yourself. Rant and rage until you are exhausted, or until you laugh at yourself.

You hate your brother: God is there, tell Him the truth, be as honest as those old Hebrews: "Routed, dishonoured, be they who delight in harm to me!" (Psalm 40:14, Moffatt). Pray God, He should punish your brother, torture him, help you to defeat him. Try to be one with God, the old God of vengeance. He will help you, if not in killing your enemy, then otherwise. Look: during all your rage, listening to your furious prayer, God was there, His presence encompassed you like the calm, creative smile of a father who knows that his child will spend his fury and then discover the truth and find the right way. Certainly you will find the right way, but only when you have spent your force, honestly and thoroughly, in rage and fury or complaint and despair. It will take weeks or months; you may have to travel the long way through the whole Old Testament, not just through a few Psalms of hatred and vengeance. And finally you will meet the God of the inner storms: "smoke fumed from his nostrils, and scorching fire from his lips, that kindled blazing coals, as down he came on the bending sky, the storm-cloud at his feet" (Psalm 18:8, 9, Moffatt). It is a nightmare more real than anything you have ever seen in the outer world. But it is not yet real enough. The highest reality emerges out of the fire in complete calm. We may realize it for a moment beyond space and time: the center itself. And at last "What is old has gone, the new has come" (II Cor. 5:17, Moffatt). The new is "God's peace that surpasses all our dreams." (Phil. 4:7, Moffatt.)

Thus we combine the old practice of "the presence of God," well known in the tradition of meditation and prayer, with the new practice of depth-psychology, well known in modern literature. The result is "confessional meditation."

Much unconscious, unexpected material will come to light; facts, tendencies, emotions, capacities, and power. It may take time, weeks and perhaps months, but it will happen. Forgotten scenes will be recalled, people and relations will appear in a different light. More important, of course, than the accumulation of material is its new evaluation and its application to our future. Grudge will change into compassion and hatred into love. Destructive tendencies will give way to newly discovered creative capacities. Our unlived life, thus released from its prison, wants to be lived. We are dimly aware, during this time, of the primitiveness and immaturity of our new desires and ideas; yet the same regression which enabled us to unearth the unconscious power now makes it difficult to refrain from its immediate use. No mistake, however, would be worse than this. Confessional meditation without continence, fasting, voluntary privation, is doomed to failure. Express your hatred or love, your greed or envy, before the face of God; but do not express them to the people whom you hate or love. This is the best way to discover more or deeper hatred or love, and to draw nearer to the real center.

You may find that your passionate love for Miss A. a week later turns into more primitive passion for Aunt B., then into a dizzying longing for your mother, and finally into awe and adoration for the terrifying Great Mother whom you did not know until you met her in your meditation. If in the meantime you had married Miss A. you would have deceived her, because your love was merely projected; and you would have stopped your own inner development. Not even your unconscious tie with Aunt B. would have come to light, unless you had divorced your pseudo-wife, A.

Our repressed drives, when they come to consciousness, are primitive, undifferentiated and powerful, like young hippopotami. Not to satisfy them is a heroic task, presupposing some training in the old and almost forgotten art of fasting. Therefore, when you set out on the road of self-education learn how to fast—not only with regard to eating too much (any good dietician can help you to learn that) but also with regard to some of your other bad habits. We not only eat and drink and smoke too much: we also talk too much, read too much, write too much; we are too busy satisfying our petty needs. If you like to smoke, stop it, and you will meet with "the beasts in the desert." And when you have the first great dream, and, stunned by its appalling colors, would like to tell your friends or husband or wife about it—stop! Fast! Refrain from gossip! If you betray the secrets of the soul no further secret will be entrusted to you. "Men will have to account on the day of judgment for every light word they utter" (Matt. 12:36, Moffatt).

Sometimes, however, the urge is so strong that the happiness of our whole life seems to depend on the fulfillment of this new and passionate desire. And still it is a merely transferred or projected desire. We are still far from the real center. We are shaken by the earthquake or the storm; we do not yet hear the still small voice. Then we need all the faith and all the courage we can muster. Because here we are at the point where we may understand one of the deepest truths of Christianity: "If your right eye is a hindrance to you, pluck it out and throw it away" (Matt. 5:29, Moffatt). Conscious sacrifice is required instead of unconscious repression, expressing all the anguish of unsatisfied vital needs before God, but not before our fellow-men. The childlike imperative "you must not . . ."

is replaced by the mature insight "I will not . . ." Thus
we may learn to leave "brothers or sisters or father or
mother or wife or children or lands or houses" . . .
(Matt. 19:29, Moffatt). This conscious sacrifice is what is
meant by fasting and plucking out our eye. It is an integral
part of confessional meditation.

On the other hand the necessity of self-control is not
limited to the phenomenon of transference and projection. There is no demarcation line between projected and
real love. We must take the risk of deceiving ourselves and
our beloved ones. And this danger is much greater during
the period of intense confessional work than at any other
time in human life. But the long and winding road of
self-education cannot be travelled in seclusion and soli-
tude. It has to be a part of our normal activity. We have
to live in the world, and its demands, satisfactions and disappointments are an integral contribution to our psychological research. We should refrain—at least during periods of crisis—from important decisions and from strong
emotional reactions towards the outer world. But we
should study this world and study our reactions towards
it, and even sometimes try, in the sense of an experiment,
to do something against our habit-patterns or beyond our
usual self-control.

This experimental method has been used in a rather
superficial way by Alfred Adler, and termed "positive
training." It provides a practical possibility of utmost importance if we combine it with confessional meditation and
apply to it the "practice of the presence of God." The
method then becomes an unerring test for what we mean

by "presence"; it becomes at once stimulus and technique for further training in outer life, and a source of valuable material for the exploration of our unconscious mind. The psychological question which determines the method is this: is the entity whose presence controls our behavior really God, or is it something else, another value, an idol, or just our Ego? The method therefore may be called: "the practice of the presence of whom?"

Imagine you discover during your psychological morning confession that you are a sheep in a wolf's skin. You behave like a wild beast; your friends are afraid of your irritability. But deep down in your heart you are kind and mild, you want peace and harmony, you want to be a Christian, and if some one should strike you on the right cheek you would like to turn the other one. Nevertheless, all attempts in this direction have failed so far. And you understand: they failed because you forgot the presence of God. You are often aware of His presence at eight o'clock during your meditation. At nine o'clock, when you enter the office, you see only the girl who forgot to mail the letters; and you howl like a wolf.

This time you try to do a better job. The presence of God should exclude the wolf. You try your best to keep His presence in mind. The girl, of course, forgot the letters. You smile. The telephone rings twice; it is the wrong number. Then you are out of cigarettes. Your fountain-pen breaks. And finally the girl wants a day off. You need all the strength of your inner wolf to maintain the sheep's smile. You look like the most self-conscious sheep that ever bleated. And the girl suddenly needs two days off and you give her three—remembering, spasmodically, the presence—of whom?

When you come home you should analyze this experience as carefully as possible. You may consider it as a complete failure. Very soon, however, you will find out that it is one of the most valuable contributions to your self-understanding. Who was present? Which power or entity was in control of your reactions? There was the conscious purpose not to grow impatient, and to smile at any cost. Did this imply that you wanted to be dishonest, to hide your true emotion, to disguise the wolf in the sheep's skin? No. You wanted to *be* the sheep, and you failed, because the shepherd was not there to protect you.

Now you remember: it was always like this during your childhood, and later too. If there was a protector you felt secure, you enjoyed peace and harmony, completely in the rôle of the good boy. And as soon as you felt left alone, without protection, you were on the defensive, firmly convinced that everybody was your enemy; and you had to be the howling wolf. This time, however, it was different. You knew: God is present. It was more than the theoretical insight into His omnipresence. It was a real experience, during your meditation, at eight o'clock. But why had you to fight the wolf all the time? Why did you not feel at ten as free as you had felt at eight?

You analyze further. Do you remember the vague presence, the shadowy figure in the background of your mind, at eight o'clock as well as at ten o'clock? Try to visualize him. He was something like a good great father, watching you and protecting you. And you wanted to please him.

You wanted to be his good boy. So you tried very hard to be patient and kind, checking, as it were, every minute: "I am a good boy, am I not, 'daddy' God?"

He was a childish substitute of a God, the idolized image of a commonplace father. And still you could not deceive him. You knew that he knew that you were not as good as you pretended to be. So you had to exaggerate your goodness. Your pretense was bad; you were afraid; he was angry; the whole thing became a stupid farce. You acted in the presence of an infantile idol and not in the presence of God. But now you know that even in your best meditation you are still far removed from the real center; and that you have to work through many more weeks or months until you can really "turn the other cheek" creatively and victoriously. But without this experiment you would never have known that you had been an idolater for so many years.

Without the verification in outer life all our inner progress remains questionable. And without the inner experience of new understanding, power and creativity, all our outer improvements would remain a shallow masquerade. The pendulum of religious self-education has to swing back and forth between introvert and extravert experiences, confessional meditation and positive training: this is the best way to avoid the one-sidedness and self-deceptions which always threaten our spiritual development.

IV

CONFESSIONAL MEDITATION

The methods described in the last chapter have to be applied in each case differently. The way which leads us to maturity and the special task we have to face in a given moment have to be explored almost every day anew. Our dreams, if we know how to use them, are a great help; but even if we have no dreams at all we can find our way. We should first try to locate our Ego-image, to determine whether it occupies the place of father, mother, son or daughter. (See Diagram I.) Often it may be an interesting mixture; and sometimes we may discover, for instance, that the Ego is basically "daughter" but that under certain circumstances it assumes the rôle of mother or even of father. This, then, constitutes a secondary line of Ego defenses and requires additional attention in self-education.

Since we usually transfer the repressed images onto our fellow-men we can often locate the Ego by inference from our transferences. If we are always afraid of powerful authorities our Ego must dwell in the passive (lower) half of the character chart (See Diagram II). If we are angered by the inefficiency of our employees we live our Ego-life in the active (upper) half of the chart. If we loathe tenderness and intimacies we are too masculine: the

Ego is on the right side. And if we are afraid of disharmony and misunderstanding we have developed a feminine form of egocentricity: our Ego is on the left side.

The task of self-education, however, is always a double
one. If the "feminine qualities" (tenderness, understanding, longing for harmony, the so-called "anima functions") are repressed and underdeveloped, the feminine
images, mother and girl, will be transferred onto several
people (usually but not necessarily women). One lady may
appear as a mild protective mother, though in reality she
is an egocentric go-getter; and another may be seen as a
sensual and greedy vampire though objectively she is an
average person. These transferences present serious tasks
for our self-education and it will be difficult enough to get
rid of our egocentric eye-glasses.

On the other hand we can be certain that in such a case
of repressed femininity the masculine functions, corresponding to the images of father and boy, will be disturbed, too. They will probably be overdeveloped, in order
to compensate for the deficiency of the opposite side. If
the person is a man he may be unaware, for a long time,
of his exaggerated "masculinity." Indeed he may consider
it a virtue; but many of his mistakes and frustrations will
be due to his onesidedness. If the person is a woman this
form of egocentricity will be more evident—and vice versa.

Looking at Diagrams III-VI we may decide first that
one of them, let us say No. III, applies to our special problem: we have to face our "Giants." Then, however, it is
very likely that one day we will discover the opposite
problem as well: half-consciously and furtively we may

bully and maltreat those who are weaker than we. Thus while applying one of the diagrams practically we should at least theoretically ask ourselves how far the opposite diagram could be applied, too.

The following diagrams serve a double purpose. They

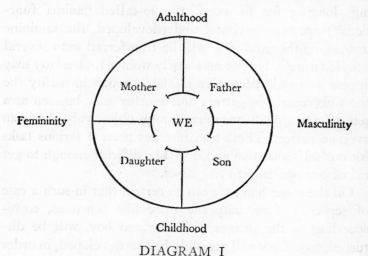

DIAGRAM I
THE ORIGINAL WE-EXPERIENCE
(See Part Two, Chapter III, Section 2: "The Inner We-Group)

illustrate the psychological facts described in Part Two of this book; and they provide some assistance for those who try to practice confessional meditation. The commentary which accompanies them is therefore divided into two sections. The first part may be read when the diagrams are studied as illustrations of the theoretical explanations. The second part should be carefully considered when they are used as charts for the "journey through the seething seas of the unconscious." However, the reader should never forget that the human mind does not exist in space. Its element is time. No picture or diagram, no configuration in space, can therefore be more than a poor crutch. It helps us somewhat if we are able to move along anyhow; but it fails us if we rely too much upon it.

The Original We-Experience (Diagram I)

1. Diagram I represents first the "ideal family," four people, two adults and two children, two males and two females, related to each other as indicated by the four sections of the outer circle as father, mother, son and daughter. The typical attitudes of the four people, and their experiences of fatherhood, motherhood, boyhood and girlhood, provide the basis of all collective images. The inmost circle, labelled "We," denotes the "tribal consciousness" as expressed in myths, habits, collective ideas, judgments, sympathies and antipathies. The contents of this tribal consciousness may or may not remain individually unconscious; the individual will act according to them anyhow, which means that he will serve the interest of the group rather than his personal interest.

At the same time the same diagram represents the inner structure, the imagery, of each of the four members of the group. The We-Psychology maintains that the inner life of the group and the inner life of each one of its members can be represented by the same diagram. The child finds already in his half-conscious mind the images of the "wise old man" and the "great mother." He does not yet understand them, but he trusts and loves their representatives in the outer world; and he knows that one day he will be one of them himself. Therefore the healthy child feels neither insecurity nor inferiority. He is a well balanced but largely unconscious organ of a well balanced but only vaguely conscious social organism: the family. This is the "Original We-experience."

Each member of the group accepts one of the four images as his leading image (which after the "breach of the We" would become his Ego-image), and uses the other three as "contact-images." They enable him to understand and love the three other members of the group. The father, for instance, should feel responsible for the whole group, the group being his central value, as represented by the "We-center" of the diagram. The Father image, upper right section, should be his leading image, representing masculinity and leadership. He should not forget, however, what childhood means, nor should femininity be missing in his inner structure.

2. Try to find out how much or how little of the "Original We-experience" has survived in your own case. Consciously you may be a nonconformist or even a rebel, and still you may discover some family pride ("we, the Smiths, do not do that") or some dependence on your cultural background ("we Southerners are different"). Many collective likes and dislikes and ready-made patterns of reactions control our behavior; they remain unconscious though operative until some outer criticism or inner self-observation raises them into consciousness. They are "remainders of the Original We."

Their contents may be right or wrong, questionable or plainly obsolete (for instance, our aversion towards a certain smell, our preference for a special landscape, a racial prejudice, etc). It may or may not be misused in the service of later egocentric goals. Our task here is neither to

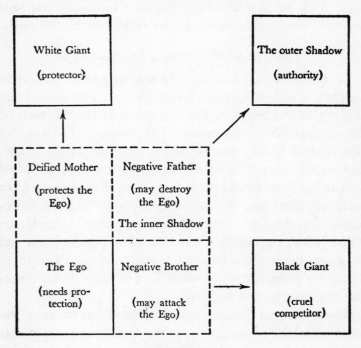

DIAGRAM II
THE EGOCENTRIC GROUP
(See Part Two, Chapter IV: "Disintegration")

This diagram showing the Ego in the lower left-hand corner represents only one of the four possible cases. The others, with the Ego in the other three corners, may easily be constructed according to the given example. (The four possible positions of the Ego constitute the four forms of egocentricity, described as Star, Nero, Gaby and Clinging Vine in the author's *How Character Develops*.)

judge nor to change them. We should only find out how far they are based on collective images and racial instincts rather than on conscious teaching and individual experience. And we should raise them into consciousness, rendering them flexible means in the service of higher goals.

The Egocentric Group (Diagram II)

1. The group of four squares has superseded the circle (squares symbolizing egocentric rigidity). The central circle, the We-experience, has disappeared: the "Breach of the original We" has occurred. The image of the daughter (lower left hand corner) has become the Ego image, though the person in question may be a boy, an adult woman, or even an old man. The other three images have been repressed into the unconscious as far as they represented functions and qualities of the person himself: he cannot take responsibility (adulthood is missing) nor can he stand disharmony (masculinity is missing). The three dotted squares represent unconscious images, which consequently have turned negative.

The repressed images are then transferred onto the other members of the group, not in their original and natural form, but rather in an exaggerated and primitive shape. One person (whether man or woman) is honored with the task of protecting the Ego: he has to play the rôle of the "White Giant." Another one is pushed into the place of an angry and unjust father: he becomes the "Ego's Shadow." A third is considered the inimical brother, a cruel and dangerous competitor. We call him the "Black Giant."

Imagine four egocentric people, each one representing one corner of the original square and transferring the other rigid and distorted images on the other members of the group. The result is a ghostly "dance macabre" of four people who pretend to love each other, but who do not know who they are.

2. Find out where your Ego and your Shadow are. Our basic pattern of egocentricity is determined by our goal, the Ego-image, and its opposite: the thing that we are most afraid of, the Ego's Shadow, the "abyss," the unbearable situation. It is represented by the egocentric caricature of the opposite image (the "egocentric daughter" would rather die than assume responsibility and make sacrifices). The Ego-image is often quite conscious, while the Shadow remains unknown; in other cases the Shadow is well known and the Ego-image remains unconscious. But we should not forget that most of us have developed a rather intricate policy of life with interwoven features of all four images. The question then is which Ego-pattern is the basic one: it is always the one that conditions the opposite image to be the Shadow.

The next task is the discovery of the virtues behind our vices. As far as you happen to be an egocentric "stepmother," whether you are man or woman, you will find that behind your egocentric vanity and striving for recognition you have developed some good objective qualities which are characteristic of an ideal mother. You like harmony, you understand the needs of your fellow-men and you know how to satisfy them.

We should not throw away the baby with the bath. We

should not fight against our Ego-pattern indiscriminately. If our Ego is located in the place of the "Son," we enjoy our long training in renunciation and our successful disci-

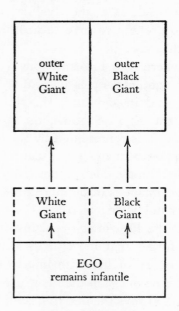

DIAGRAM III

CONQUERING THE GIANTS

The Journey of Those
Who Have Remained
(partly   or   entirely)
Infantile

pline in asceticism. But we should learn to use it or not to use it, freely and according to circumstances. The father, and even the egocentric one, likes responsibility; the ego-

centric sissy has developed the most subtle ways of diplomacy. They should use these "virtues" for the sake of
the We-group rather than in the service of the Ego.

Conquering the Giants (Diagram III)

1. The two foregoing diagrams (I and II) refer to the
problems of diagnosis; the four following ones are related
to the way out as we may achieve it by means of confessional meditation. We describe the "journey" in four significant directions, leaving it to the imagination of the
reader to work out the special combinations and complica-
tions which may be needed in his own case. Since the Ego
usually represents a mixture of several images it is advisable to begin our practical training in terms of attitudes
and functions rather than in terms of images. The word
"childhood" here covers the common attitudes of boy and
girl; "adulthood" those of man and woman; "masculinity" those of the two male and "femininity" those of
the two female members of the group. The exact diagnosis of the location of the Ego will then be worked out
gradually while the egocentric attitudes are already dwin-
dling away under the impact of a good-humored self-
analysis. (Do not moralize: by condemning yourself you
keep the Ego alive!)

The inner Shadow will then be a mixture of the two
opposite images; and the "outer Shadows," the transferences of the inner Shadow onto people in the outer world,
will be a mixture too. The transferences of the Shadow (in
the proper sense; see Part Two, Chapter IV, Section 1)
and of the Black Giant, which appear as two different fig-

ures on Diagram II, are in practice so frequently blended that the two words can be used almost synonymously.

The lower rectangle represents the Ego of a person who remained infantile. The dotted squares are his repressed and therefore degenerated images of adults, the "White Giant" being too white, the "Black Giant" too black, and both being superhumanly big, almost like angels and devils. This unfortunate inner structure is based on painful experiences in early childhood and connected with old collective dreams about the terrible Great Mother or the father Saturn, who eat their children. This image has provoked its own counterpart, the "White Giant," because life would have been impossible without this remedy. The more the child fears the doctor, or the dog, or the dark, the more he needs the mother or the aunt to protect him. The outer experience of being spoiled is always connected with some collective image of a great protector.

Both images are transferred, later, onto all kinds of authorities: boss, teacher, minister, government, church, God, or even husband or wife. Sometimes one person carries both images. That person may be the White Giant while he praises us, but turns black as soon as he frowns. In this case it is a matter of life and death to keep him white. In reality he may be green or red, and rather small; we see him black or white and always gigantic, according to our distorted and colored eyeglasses.

2. We should write out and meditate on a list of all our black and white giants, with all their good and bad qualities, as we see them. The changes of color and size and especially the double transference, the same giant

being alternately white and black, will convince us that the source of this evil is to be found in our own unlived life. We should be what we think they are. Moreover, we are unconsciously what our consciousness erroneously ascribes to them. And we cannot get rid of the Black Giant and the fear which his image creates, unless we give up our claim to protection and our longing for the White Giant.

The White Giant, especially if we project this image on God, is very bad: it prevents us from growing up, becoming independent and assuming our own responsibility. The Black Giant, even if we do not project this image, makes us suffer and therefore is extremely helpful, forcing us into our own crisis. What we deem evil is really good, and what we call good is very bad. This insight is an important milestone on the road of our inner journey: the Ego valuation is replaced by a more objective, more central understanding of the relativity of all inner values.

Thus we realize that we have to integrate the images of the Black as well as of the White Giant. The inner way is to go back in our imagination to the earliest scenes with them which we can find, either in memory or in mere fantasy. Be the child once more, frightened to death by your father's severity, or spoiled by the sentimentality of your aunt. And at the same time be there as the adult that you are, or even wiser than you are in reality. You will feel the child's anguish and fear, or, when spoiled, his shallow smugness. At the same time the adult's resentment will rise in angry waves. You will realize an anger, unknown so far, because it was carefully repressed. Now be honest. Tell your father or your aunt who are there without being there how you feel. They have poisoned your life, murdered your creativity. The terrific power of revenge will surge up from the unconscious and flood your consciousness. You may be carried away by your "sacred wrath"; but remember: God is still there, too.

Drag your father or your aunt before His tribunal. Listen to what He may tell you. He certainly will not be the White Giant that you want Him to be. He will disappoint you. And still you may sense His smile. Then, bewildered by rage and shame, you will recognize that you are obsessed by an image, playing a rôle, convinced of your own righteousness, exactly as your father or your aunt were playing a rôle, serving an image, being convinced of their moral right. You are certainly as weak and blind as your aunt or your father have been. You are equally human, obsessed by the same collective images, caught in the same collective misery. So you may shake hands, and forgive one another.

Then prepare the next step, the extravert part of the way. But keep in mind where you are on the road. The destructive power, fury, and revenge have given you a new experience of strength and almost of joy. All cowardice, all inferiority feeling were gone; you realized for a moment what your ancestors would have called the sacred rage of the battlefield. Your buried talent, your unlived life, arose from the dead; you were integrated for a minute, though on a primitive level of consciousness. This regression brought you close to the center, and its creative power can catapult you wherever you want to go. You can use your new strength for constructive development. You have unearthed your buried sword: try to reforge it into a plough. And you will see that God has forgiven you as you have forgiven your aunt or your father.

At the next opportunity face the person on whom you transfer the image of the Black Giant. Remember that you are not afraid of *him* but of your inner image which you transfer on him, and that you can be (and indeed have been) this image yourself. If necessary go fast, within ten seconds, through the whole gamut of emotions and insights: fear, fury, sacred wrath, bewilderment and mutual forgiveness. Then tell him as kindly and objectively as possible what you have to say; talk business with him; and keep your inner secrets for yourself.

The task is very similar if you have to meet the black situation, the abyss, instead of the Black Giant. (For instance, in the case of a speech inhibition: try to speak, but not before you have unearthed the roots of the evil). Do the impossible thing, assume responsibility, make your decision, become the leader, expose yourself to criticism and failure. But choose only small steps. Do not expect too much. And if you fail, as you probably will do nine times out of ten, go back to your confessional meditation, face once more your Black and White Giants, try to unearth more fear or hatred or revengefulness, and try to realize a deeper degree of forgiveness.

Exploring the Dog-House (Diagram IV)

1. Here the situation is the opposite of that in Diagram III. The Ego-image is high up in the air; the Shadow is consequently represented by a situation rather than by a

person: it is helplessness, withdrawal, failure, defeat. Consciously this person may say he has never experienced defeat, that he has been a splendid success all through his

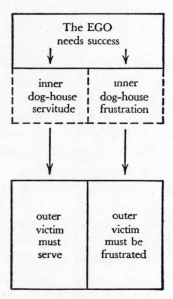

DIAGRAM IV

Exploring the Dog-
house

The Journey of Those
Who Have Been Spoiled
(partly or completely)
by Outer Success

life. In early childhood, however, he must have had this experience and found it so unbearable that he repressed even the slightest reminder of it. His unconscious policy of life now is: to do everything to forestall defeat.

His abyss may be symbolized by a dog house. But the only way in which it appears outwardly is its transference on other people. His inner dog house, repressed and abhorred, provides the refined and almost fiendish skill of putting others into their own dog house. He needs victims. That seems to be the only thing which makes him feel that he is not a victim himself. He teases, blames, ridicules, but does not allow anybody to pay back in kind. He wants to be served, but does not serve himself. He cannot even apologize or say "thanks," so much is he afraid of any possible humiliation.

2. If such is your case, little can be done as long as you are satisfied with your life. You are using only half of your possibilities, but you cannot change this situation unless you suffer. Life, however, will draw you closer and closer to your own dog house; your good luck will fail you, and then your better luck may begin, with nightmares and nervous jitters.

Try to discover your early experience of the dog house. Gather all the evidence and draw conclusions, like Sherlock Holmes. The crime has happened; reconstruct its circumstances as carefully as you can. Go in your imagination through the presumable Hell of that childhood experience, and try to anticipate the possible Hell of tomorrow. The two series of pictures will help each other. Imagine that some one does to you what you like to do to your victims. And always look for the most disagreeable situation: this is probably what has been done to you.

If you have found your abyss, go through it in your meditation, feeling as you did in childhood that something "impossible" happens, and realizing at the same time as an adult that there is no real loss. You are ridiculed, exploited, defeated; it is true, you may lose your "face," your reputation, your glamor—indeed you lose your mask, and your real face, your human nature appears. You are miserable but honest, now, without pretense and without claim; frank, plain and naked; completely alone, forsaken, enslaved; but all your humiliation exists only as long as you fight against it. Accept it——and finally you cannot help accepting it—and it is gone. Then you discover the essential secret of the dog house: there is no dog house at all.

Meanwhile everyday life will give you many a chance to check your inner progress by outer experiences. Do not shun the humiliating situations, face them, exploit them for your inner development. Allow yourself to be teased, ridiculed, exploited; learn that you can survive without losing your human dignity, and that you can serve without feeling enslaved. Learn that failure and defeat are part of human life as well as success and victory. And the rhythm of contraction and expansion will encourage you, foreshadowing death and resurrection. Thus, in complete loneliness you may discover that most people, knowingly or unknowingly, are as alone as you are. You will discover their real faces behind their masks; you will love them; and finally you will find the great brotherhood of suffering mankind.

If you succeed in breaking the spell of the Giants and of the dog house you will be able to say with St. Paul that you are "initiated into the secret for all sorts and conditions of life, for plenty and for hunger, for prosperity and

for privations" (Phil. 4:12, Moffatt). If it is not so, go
back to your confessional meditation and begin anew.

Awakening "Sleeping Beauty" (Diagram V)

1. The person represented in Diagram V has developed
the egocentric caricature of masculinity as his Ego-image.
It can express itself in terms of pure intellectualism and

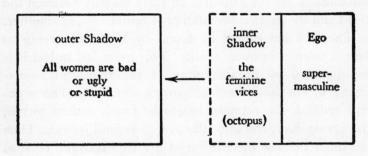

DIAGRAM V

AWAKENING "SLEEPING BEAUTY"

The Journey of Those Who Reject Tenderness and Neglect
Harmony

moralism, or as super-orderliness, pedantry, and fastid-
iousness, or as coarseness, cruelty and brutality. Women
are despised, misused and sometimes dreaded. All this is
bad enough if the person is a man. If it happens to be a
woman, her Ego is doubly deviated; she is an "animus-
ridden" lady. The typical dream of these people who do
not dare to expose themselves emotionally is nakedness.

The "anima," the feminine image, is repressed into the
unconscious and degenerated into some dreadful and

loathsome collective symbol such as the serpent, the vampire, the octopus. These images are later transferred onto almost every woman in the outer world, so that they appear to be "ugly, mean, base, treacherous, shallow, stupid, or enigmatical, incomprehensible, unfathomable." All "womanish" reactions are denounced; and one half of human life is sacrificed. The basis of this unfortunate one-sidedness is always of course an early tragedy between the child and the first representative of femininity, his mother.

The way out cannot be found by loving or trying to love a woman in outer reality. This must fail unless it is accompanied by the discovery of the repressed anima-image within the individual's own unconscious. The negative symbol, the octopus, has to be faced, and its virtue, the loving Eve, has to be discovered behind its vice. Thus the inner defense mechanism of the Ego becomes useless. Its fear of the octopus, its loathing and disgust are recognized as the disguised creative power of the real center: even Eve is a child of God, and a beautiful one. Then the rigid Ego disappears; its counterpart, the Shadow, is integrated; loathing is superseded by love, and the new life can develop.

2. The way through confessional meditation is in this case characterized by the word relaxation. Give up your self-control. All your discipline and concentration are mere Ego-defense and therefore self-deception. Try to be honest: let come to consciousness what lurks and lures in your unconscious depths, though it be as ugly and obscene as the witch Baubo or as beautiful and pernicious as Lilith.

The symbols may be indistinct and changing: Eve, Venus, Sleeping Beauty, Cinderella, witches, queens and madonnas may visit you in dreams and fantasies. The emotional gamut will prove to be rather simple: loathing will be replaced by lure; we will feel our loneliness, not yet being courageous enough to woo, because that would mean to admit our longing, our unhappiness, weakness and helplessness. Then we may recognize that just this is human life, and suddenly the power of love will push us ahead like a tempest. We are servants of the real center. We have to obey. And the unspeakable joy and courage of a super-individual passion will make us humble and strong at the same time.

The way is the same for men and women. Men will find that the Eve-image teaches them the values, the beauty and the dignity of womanhood. The more they develop Eve, the more they have to become Adam, and to replace their Ego-image by true masculinity. The woman, discovering her inner Eve-image, suddenly learns what it means to be feminine. She renounces her former Ego-image which was too masculine, and finds that the male qualities are useful to her if they remain secondary, and that they help her to understand and to enjoy her newly found counterpart in the outer world, the real Adam.

The introvert way should be paralleled by outer experiences. The steps usually are three: first we should learn to reveal and to express appropriately our tender emotions, without too much modesty or shame. Second we should learn to woo, even if there is no or almost no chance of success. This includes the art of giving gifts which meet the partner's taste, exploring his real needs and capacities, especially those which he does not know himself, and helping him to live a fuller, and more creative kind of life.

The third step is the final test of love: where there is love there can be no disgust. The mother does not mind her babe's dirty diapers. Two lovers like to eat with one spoon. The good nurse, the real physician, are not deterred by the odor of rotting pus. And, at the Lord's Supper, do you like to share the communion cup with your Christian brothers? Hygiene, of course, forces us to disinfect the cup; but behind hygiene hides our lack of love.

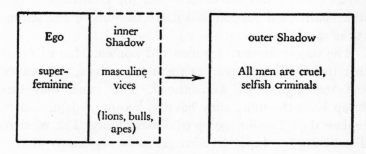

DIAGRAM VI

ORGANIZING THE ORGANIZER

The Journey of Those Who Are Afraid of Disharmony, Disapproval and Privation

Organizing the Organizer (Diagram VI)

1. Diagram VI represents a person whose Ego-image shows merely feminine qualities, though it may have a masculine name. The individual, whether man or woman, is a sissy, not balanced by masculine traits. All masculinity has been repressed into the unconscious and has degenerated into primitive collective symbols such as lions, tigers, dogs, bulls, horses, apes, criminals and especially

burglars. To be chased by a beast or frightened by an intruder is a common dream of all effeminate people.

The unconscious image of the intruder is then transferred onto friends and enemies alike. The "anima"-character is therefore soft and kind, but suspicious and cowardly. And his repressed aggressiveness often finds an outlet in unconscious cruelty (corresponding to the unconscious sentimentality of the animus-character). The lack of animus-qualities is most obvious in the person's incapacity to organize time and energy, his carelessness with regard to money, his lack of discrimination, and his tendency to indulge in all kinds of weakness.

What these people need is discipline and organization, but they cannot develop them as long as they are afraid of sacrifice. The power of organization is the capacity to say "no," to face disapproval and disharmony, and to overcome them by an effort at conscious creativity. This power, however, has been transformed into destructive and primitive tendencies. The task, therefore, is to integrate these tendencies, to raise them into consciousness and to transform them into positive "virtues."

2. The origin of this repression is always connected with a father problem. The confessional meditation should therefore begin with remembrances concerning the father (or the mother, if she was the more masculine type). What did we learn about masculinity? How much tenacity and fortitude, how many Spartan and Stoic virtues did we develop? Now we must make up for what we skipped in early childhood. Now we have to face first the inner burglars, bulls and lions and later the outer opponents. This is similar to, but not identical with, the task of facing the

Black Giants (Diagram III). The giant is our superior, and stronger than we are; the burglar is cruel and malicious, but he may be rather small and limited in his

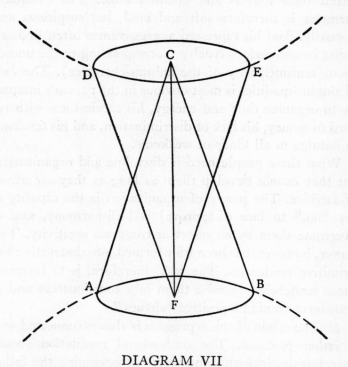

DIAGRAM VII
THE NATURAL AND THE SPIRITUAL WE-EXPERIENCE
(The Way to Maturity)

strength. It is his inhuman recklessness which renders him terrible. Often, however, the two images are combined as a giant intruder.

The emotional aspect of our reeducation begins with fright or horror, leads through hatred and cruelty—now our own primitive cruelty, taken over from the checked and astonished opponent—and it ends in a completely new attitude towards suffering, our own as well as that of other people. What seemed to be unbearable is now easily sustained, and even death has lost its repulsiveness. The development is from horror via hatred to heroism.

The extravert part of the way may begin with modest experiments in "Spartanism." Fasting, saying "no" to ourselves first, later on to friends and even to superiors. Renouncing our favorite distractions; refraining from caresses and (very important!) from gossiping and telling lies. Thus we may train ourselves to make sacrifices; we may prepare the sacrifice of our time, strength, health and lives; and finally we may meet the great test of maturity: if necessary, to inflict, consciously and conscientiously, pain and sacrifice upon our most beloved friends.

The Natural and the Spiritual We-Experience
(Diagram VII)

1. Diagrams III to VI deal with the reintegration of the one-sided and eccentric personality. There is no doubt that the new equilibrium can be found only on a higher level of consciousness, the person being individually conscious of and responsible for the whole group to which he belongs. This progress is usually reached through the failure of our eccentric deviations; but it would take place, and even more markedly, if no deviation had occurred at all. The first task, correcting our eccentricity, corresponds

to the medieval idea of "purgation"; the second task, achieving the higher consciousness, is "illumination." Both, as we said, are practically interwoven; theoretically, however, it is useful time and again to separate them.

Moreover, Diagrams III to VI refer to egocentricity; they are of no—or almost no—use in cases of idolatry. The development described in Diagram VII, on the other hand, applies to all kinds of sham religion. Our Idols, high as they may be, are still deviated nature; their spirituality is spurious. And the true Spirit, the Spirit of the living God, will put us to a test and destroy all such delusions. The Idols will fail us when we need them most urgently, just as health and money and friends and all other natural values will fail.

Consider the cone ABC: it represents the natural life of the human being, including the lower or tribal consciousness as well as the Ego-consciousness of the civilized individual. Its goal is self-preservation. Time, however, symbolized by the line FC, leading upward, brings about the gradual decrease of the cone's perimeter and finally its end at C. Human life does not last. Individuals and groups, institutions and cultures, decay and disappear. Hence the melancholy of so many poets and philosophers. Even the best kind of life, the deepest We-feeling and the highest courage, do not alter the fact that life is doomed to die—because it is meant to change, and to rise again.

The circle AB is identical with the larger circle of Diagram I, representing the original We-group (or the member of the group who lives the group-life). The inner circle of Diagram I, the "We-center," here is the point

F, the beginning of the spiritual life as represented by the cone DEF. This "spiritual cone" increases to the same degree as the "natural cone" decreases—if the development is not disturbed by eccentric deviations which may engender the decrease of both cones at the same time.

The cone DEF represents the higher consciousness, the "maturing We-experience," the "inner light" which is given to us as a seed (point F) and is supposed to engross our earthly life increasingly until the latter vanishes completely and the former alone survives (point C). Notice that the spiritual center of the original We-group during the second half of the development encompasses the narrowing "natural cone," so that center and perimeter are exchanged. The mature personality should lead an all-embracing spiritual life which permeates and surpasses his physical existence rather than remaining its hidden center, as it used to be during the first half of his life.

2. The practical implication is that every loss in the realm of natural life could and should be an adequate gain in the realm of the spirit. Loss of money or reputation, accidents, diseases, death of our friends or relatives, and finally the visible approach of our own death—all these losses should become spiritual gains.

The progress may be achieved when the loss occurs in reality—this is the most painful way; or it may be prepared in imagination, replacing the outer event by inner growth. This psychological preparation not only decreases the pain of the actual loss but sometimes supersedes it entirely and thus helps to avoid it ("some will not taste death"). The way for the beginner, however, should be a third one: remember losses that you have not yet assimi-

lated. Do not acquiesce, do not repress your emotional reactions. If you feel resentment, bitterness, rebellion against
God or man, express it thoroughly through confessional
meditation. This is the reaction of the natural cone. Then
remember the spiritual world. Look for the center and its
possible growth. What does the natural loss mean? What
does God want you to discover, or to understand, or to do?
This question is the first beginning of your spiritual reaction.

Did the wolf chase you? Be sure he acted—without
knowing it—as the shepherd's dog. You are in the hands
of the living God, and all who know agree that this is
terrible. If you could help him to help you it would be
less painful for both of you. Indeed, all evil would cease
to be evil in the very moment that you could understand
and accept and forgive. This does not mean acquiescence.
Stop the evil-doers; they do harm to many people; and, if
you cannot stop them, exploit what they have done for
your own growth. Then it ceases to be evil to you, though
it remains evil for them.

This inner growth, the transformation of the collective
powers from the original We-structure into the structure
of the maturing We-experience, is not an action of our conscious will, though the will must cooperate; nor is it a
merely emotional process, though emotional changes are
important; nor is it an intellectual event, though the
higher understanding is usually its most significant symptom. It is a central development, including willing and
thinking and feeling alike. It is spiritual growth. It is continuing creation and therefore worth every sacrifice.

Index

INDEX

Addictions, 61
Adler, Alfred, 31
Adventurousness, 55
Alcoholism, 155 (note), 159
Allegories, 93f
Anxiety, 26, 89ff, 112

Blunders, 59f, 149ff
Breach of the We, 85ff, 132

Caesarian madness, 180
Causality, 198, 201
Christ, 68
Christian psychology, its viewpoint, 33; dualistic and monistic, 38; dynamic, 40
Clairvoyance, 73 (note), 95, 189
Clarification, 8
Confession, 118, 251
Consciousness, 82, 188f, 194
Continence, 256
Creativity, 236
Crisis, 18, 145ff, 153, 160, 213ff

Demons, 83, 96
Differentiation, 116, 120
Disintegration, 123
Dualism, 38

Education, religious, 84
Ego, 73, 77, 89, 92, 118 (note)
Energy, 54
Evil, 219f, 233, 242

Faith, 238
Fanaticism, 177

Fasting, 257
Father complex, 283
Father image, 127f
Feudalism, 115
Forgiveness, 118, 244
Freud, Sigmund, 22, 26, 31, 60, 62, 150 (note)
Fury, 73 (note)

God, 85, 192
Gods, 83, 96
Grace, 219f
Guilt, collective, 82

Habits, bad, 61
Hatred, 73 (note)
Honesty, 243

"I," the, 71
Idolatry, 44, 45, 109, 164ff
Images, 93f, 98, 100, 116, 128
Illusion, 198
Individualism, 115
Individuation, 189
Inferiority feeling, 87, 101, 119, 138, 143, 166, 172
Inhibition, 147
Integration, 123
"Isms," 184ff

Jesus, 12
Jung, C. G., 23, 118 (note)

Law of reversed effort, 156

Madonna, 94
Mars, 96, 108